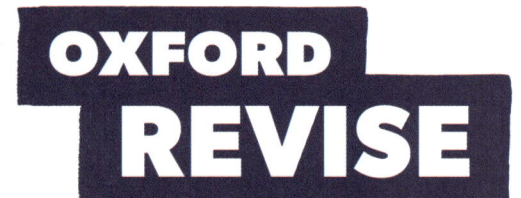

AQA GCSE MACBETH

English Literature

COMPLETE REVISION AND PRACTICE

Series Editor: Lyndsay Bawden

Graham Elsdon

Contents

 Shade in each level of the circle as you feel more confident and ready for your exam.

How to use this book — iv

Plot — 2–21

1 Act One — 2
- Knowledge
- Retrieval

2 Act Two — 6
- Knowledge
- Retrieval

3 Act Three — 10
- Knowledge
- Retrieval

4 Act Four — 14
- Knowledge
- Retrieval
- Practice

5 Act Five — 18
- Knowledge
- Retrieval

Methods — 22–29

6 Writer's methods — 22
- Knowledge
- Retrieval

Characters — 30–55

7 Macbeth — 30
- Knowledge
- Retrieval

8 Lady Macbeth — 36
- Knowledge
- Retrieval

9 The witches — 42
- Knowledge
- Retrieval

10 Macduff — 46
- Knowledge
- Retrieval

11 Banquo — 50
- Knowledge
- Retrieval

12 Duncan and Malcolm — 53
- Knowledge
- Retrieval

Themes	56–85

13 Ambition — 56
- Knowledge ⊖
- Retrieval ⊖

14 Power — 61
- Knowledge ⊖
- Retrieval ⊖

15 Death and violence — 66
- Knowledge ⊖
- Retrieval ⊖

16 Deception — 71
- Knowledge ⊖
- Retrieval ⊖

17 Suffering and guilt — 76
- Knowledge ⊖
- Retrieval ⊖

18 Evil and the supernatural — 81
- Knowledge ⊖
- Retrieval ⊖

Exam Skills and Sample Answers	86–97

- Knowledge ⊖
- Retrieval ⊖

Exam Practice	98–113

- Practice ⊖

How to use this book

This book uses a three-step approach to revision: **Knowledge**, **Retrieval**, and **Practice**. It is important that you do all three; they work together to make your revision effective.

Knowledge

Knowledge comes first. Each chapter is divided into **Knowledge Organisers**. These are clear, easy-to-understand, concise summaries of the content that you need to know for your exam. The information is organised to show how one idea flows into the next so you can learn how everything is tied together.

Sample answers and examiner's comments are also provided where appropriate to help you understand what makes a good answer.

REMEMBER

The Remember box offers useful guidance.

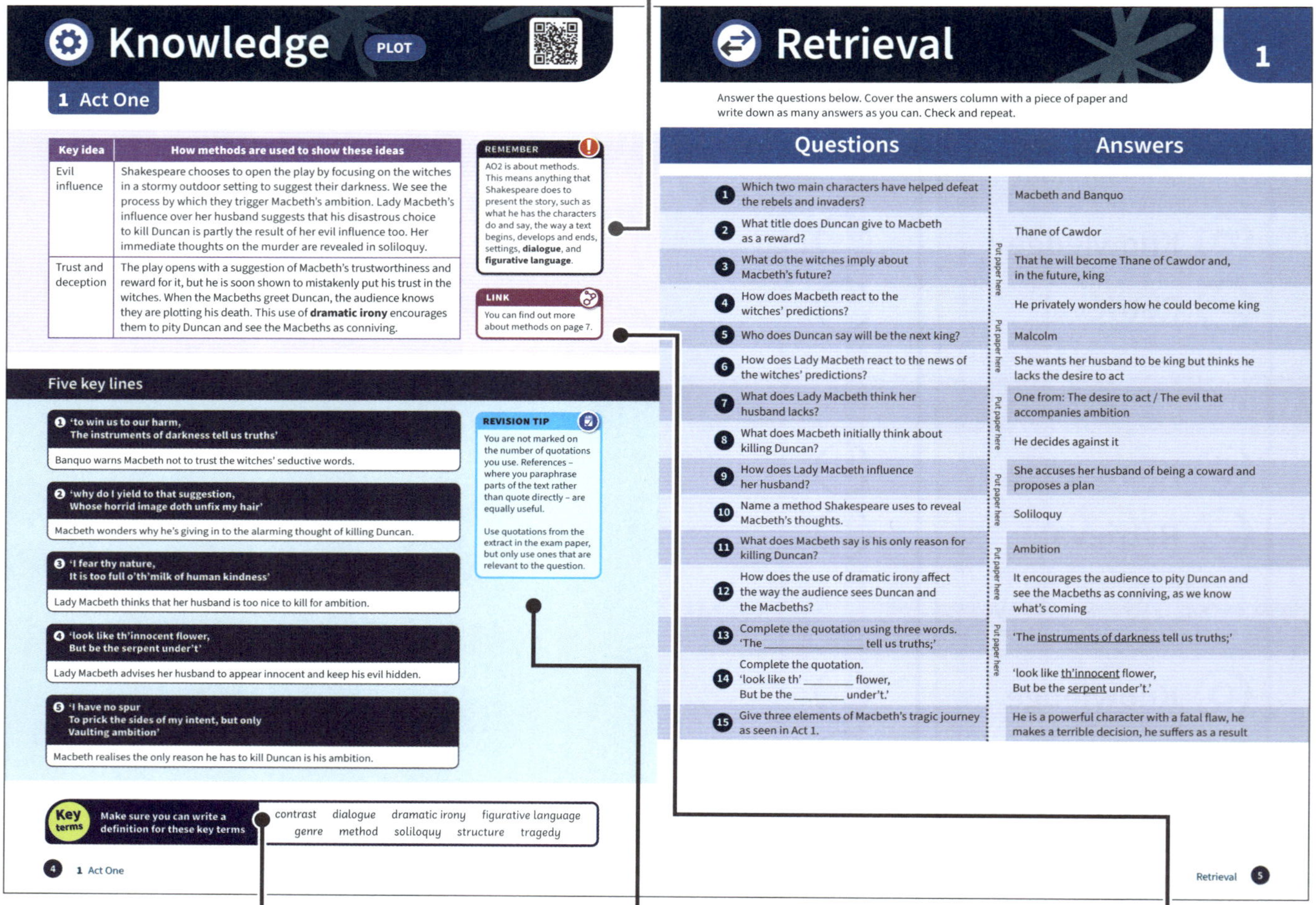
Knowledge PLOT

1 Act One

Key idea	How methods are used to show these ideas
Evil influence	Shakespeare chooses to open the play by focusing on the witches in a stormy outdoor setting to suggest their darkness. We see the process by which they trigger Macbeth's ambition. Lady Macbeth's influence over her husband suggests that his disastrous choice to kill Duncan is partly the result of her evil influence too. Her immediate thoughts on the murder are revealed in soliloquy.
Trust and deception	The play opens with a suggestion of Macbeth's trustworthiness and reward for it, but he is soon shown to mistakenly put his trust in the witches. When the Macbeths greet Duncan, the audience knows they are plotting his death. This use of **dramatic irony** encourages them to pity Duncan and see the Macbeths as conniving.

REMEMBER

AO2 is about methods. This means anything that Shakespeare does to present the story, such as what he has the characters do and say, the way a text begins, develops and ends, settings, **dialogue**, and **figurative language**.

LINK

You can find out more about methods on page 7.

Five key lines

1 'to win us to our harm,
The instruments of darkness tell us truths'

Banquo warns Macbeth not to trust the witches' seductive words.

2 'why do I yield to that suggestion,
Whose horrid image doth unfix my hair'

Macbeth wonders why he's giving in to the alarming thought of killing Duncan.

3 'I fear thy nature,
It is too full o'th'milk of human kindness'

Lady Macbeth thinks that her husband is too nice to kill for ambition.

4 'look like th'innocent flower,
But be the serpent under't'

Lady Macbeth advises her husband to appear innocent and keep his evil hidden.

5 'I have no spur
To prick the sides of my intent, but only
Vaulting ambition'

Macbeth realises the only reason he has to kill Duncan is his ambition.

REVISION TIP

You are not marked on the number of quotations you use. References – where you paraphrase parts of the text rather than quote directly – are equally useful.

Use quotations from the extract in the exam paper, but only use ones that are relevant to the question.

Key terms Make sure you can write a definition for these key terms

contrast dialogue dramatic irony figurative language genre method soliloquy structure tragedy

4 1 Act One

Retrieval 1

Answer the questions below. Cover the answers column with a piece of paper and write down as many answers as you can. Check and repeat.

	Questions	Answers
1	Which two main characters have helped defeat the rebels and invaders?	Macbeth and Banquo
2	What title does Duncan give to Macbeth as a reward?	Thane of Cawdor
3	What do the witches imply about Macbeth's future?	That he will become Thane of Cawdor and, in the future, king
4	How does Macbeth react to the witches' predictions?	He privately wonders how he could become king
5	Who does Duncan say will be the next king?	Malcolm
6	How does Lady Macbeth react to the news of the witches' predictions?	She wants her husband to be king but thinks he lacks the desire to act
7	What does Lady Macbeth think her husband lacks?	One from: The desire to act / The evil that accompanies ambition
8	What does Macbeth initially think about killing Duncan?	He decides against it
9	How does Lady Macbeth influence her husband?	She accuses her husband of being a coward and proposes a plan
10	Name a method Shakespeare uses to reveal Macbeth's thoughts.	Soliloquy
11	What does Macbeth say is his only reason for killing Duncan?	Ambition
12	How does the use of dramatic irony affect the way the audience sees Duncan and the Macbeths?	It encourages the audience to pity Duncan and see the Macbeths as conniving, as we know what's coming
13	Complete the quotation using three words. 'The ______ tell us truths;'	'The instruments of darkness tell us truths;'
14	Complete the quotation. 'look like th' ______ flower, But be the ______ under't.'	'look like th'innocent flower, But be the serpent under't.'
15	Give three elements of Macbeth's tragic journey as seen in Act 1.	He is a powerful character with a fatal flaw, he makes a terrible decision, he suffers as a result

Put paper here

Retrieval 5

Key terms Make sure you can write a definition for these key terms

The **Key terms** box highlights the key words and phrases you need to know, remember, and be able to use confidently.

REVISION TIP

Revision tips offer you helpful advice and guidance to aid your revision and help you to understand key concepts and remember them.

LINK

The Link box offers a reference to a related topic.

Retrieval

The **Retrieval questions** help you learn and quickly recall the information you've acquired. These are short questions and answers about the Knowledge Organiser content you have just revised. Cover up the answers with some paper and write down as many answers as you can from memory. Check back to the Knowledge Organisers for any you got wrong, then cover the answers and attempt all the questions again until you can answer *all* the questions correctly.

Make sure you revisit the Retrieval questions on different days to help them stick in your memory. You need to write down the answers each time, or say them out loud, for your revision to be effective.

Previous questions

Many Retrieval pages also have some **Retrieval questions** from **previous topics**. Answer these to see if you can remember the content from the earlier sections. If you get the answers wrong, go back and do the Retrieval questions for the earlier topics again.

Practice questions linked to the content you have just been revising are flagged here.

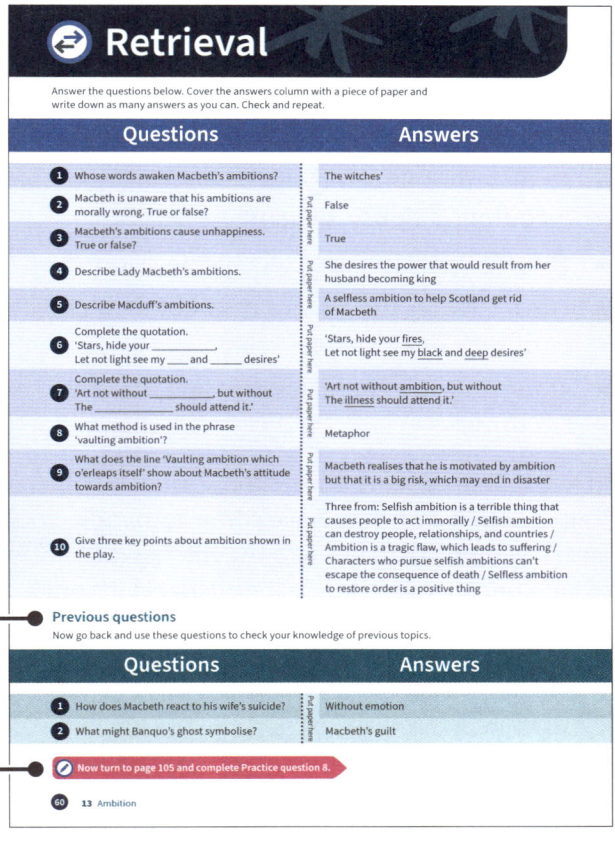

Practice

Once you are confident with the Knowledge Organisers and Retrieval questions, you can move on to the final stage: **Practice**. This can be found at the back of the book.

The **exam-style questions** in this section help you apply all the knowledge you have learned.

EXAM TIP

Exam tips show you how to interpret the questions, provide guidance on how to answer them, and give advice on how to secure as many marks as possible. Guidance is also offered on how to approach different command words.

Answers and Glossary

You can scan the QR codes at any time to access sample answers and mark schemes for the exam-style questions, a glossary containing definitions of the key terms, as well as further revision support, or go to go.oup.com/OR/GCSE/A/EngLit/Macbeth

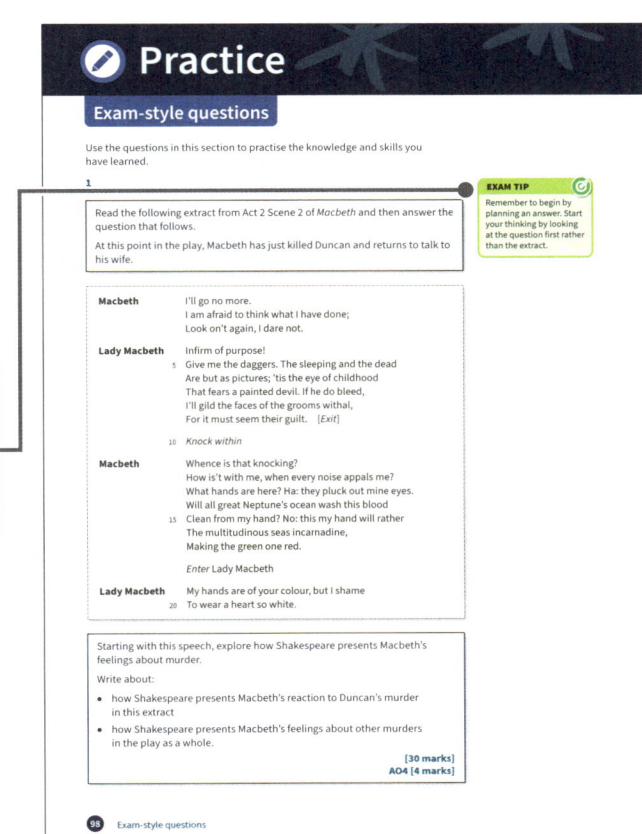

v

Knowledge — PLOT

1 Act One

Macbeth's tragic journey

Shakespeare uses the **genre** of **tragedy** to present the story of Macbeth. The following events happen in most tragedies:

- A powerful character with some good qualities has a fatal flaw, for example, ambition, jealousy, or vanity.
- The character makes a terrible decision, even though they are warned not to.
- The character suffers as a result of their choice and they come to realise the error they have made.
- At the end, the character dies and there is a sense that the world will get back to normal.

In Act 1, Shakespeare shows the start of Macbeth's tragedy. He is shown to have some admirable qualities, and is warned not to listen to the witches, but he decides to kill Duncan, even though he suspects it's not a good idea.

> **REMEMBER**
> Tragedy explores the process of a character's downfall. The focus of tragedy is on the experience of making errors and facing the consequences of them. Pinpoint the moments where warnings are ignored and consequences emerge.

> **REMEMBER**
> You don't need to explain what tragedy is in the exam – your job is to show how it relates specifically to *Macbeth* and the events of the play.

Key events

The main characters and world of the play – medieval Scotland – are introduced. Macbeth, a Scottish general, is a loyal and brave soldier, but is tempted to commit murder once he hears the predictions of the witches. We see how Lady Macbeth manipulates her husband and persuades him to kill King Duncan.

Scene 1
- Three witches decide to meet Macbeth after a battle has ended.

Scene 2
- King Duncan, King of Scotland, asks for news about the battle in which Scottish rebels, Irish invaders, and Norwegians are attacking Scotland.
- Duncan is told that two generals, Macbeth and Banquo, have helped to defeat the rebels and invaders.
- Duncan orders the death of one of the Scottish rebels, the Thane of Cawdor. The king then decides to make Macbeth the Thane of Cawdor as a reward.

Scene 3
- The witches meet Macbeth and imply that he will become Thane of Cawdor and, in the future, king; they say Banquo's sons will be kings too.
- A messenger arrives to give Macbeth the title Thane of Cawdor.
- Banquo warns Macbeth not to trust the words of the witches.
- Macbeth privately wonders how he could become king.

> **REVISION TIP**
> It is vital that you know the key events of the story and the order in which they happen. Full knowledge of the story allows you to select the most useful things to include in an answer.

> **REVISION TIP**
> Take note of how the main characters are first introduced. Does Shakespeare first show the character actively doing or saying something, or does he have another character describe them before they appear on stage?

1

Scene 4
- Duncan announces that his eldest son, Malcolm, will be the next king, and this annoys Macbeth.
- Plans are made for Duncan to travel to Macbeth's castle. Macbeth travels ahead to tell his wife, Lady Macbeth.

Scene 5
- Lady Macbeth reads a letter she has received from Macbeth telling her about the witches' predictions.
- Lady Macbeth wants her husband to be king but thinks he lacks the desire to act.
- Macbeth arrives and Lady Macbeth encourages the murder of Duncan, saying she will plan it.

Scene 6
- Duncan arrives and is greeted warmly by the Macbeths.

Scene 7
- Macbeth thinks about the murder and decides against it.
- Lady Macbeth accuses her husband of being a coward and proposes a plan.
- Macbeth changes his mind and agrees that Duncan should die.

> **REMEMBER**
> Shakespeare doesn't use a lot of stage directions or text to describe setting and the world of the play. Take note of how the values of the play's world, such as aspects of power and gender, are conveyed through speech and action.

Key ideas of Act One

Writing about the big ideas of the text is the most important aspect of your studies. But you also need to understand *how* these ideas are presented – the **methods** that Shakespeare uses to show these ideas.

Key idea	How methods are used to show these ideas
Loyalty	Shakespeare **structures** the opening of the play to establish Macbeth as trustworthy. He defends Duncan and respects his leadership. This allows the audience to see that Macbeth has admirable qualities, and see how temptation changes him as the story develops.
Ambition	Shakespeare focuses the audience's attention on how Macbeth is tempted. Once he has met the witches, we see how his desire for power is awoken. In **soliloquy**, Macbeth reflects how ambition is his only reason to kill Duncan. Shakespeare uses Banquo's cautious reaction to the witches as a **contrast** to Macbeth's.
Violence and power	Shakespeare establishes the world of the play as a violent one, where people use violence to gain and maintain power. Characters are rewarded for loyalty. Macbeth's bloodthirsty ways in battle are revealed in the opening act of the play. This alerts the audience to the ease with which he kills opponents.

> **REMEMBER**
> In English, some terms and concepts mean largely the same thing. The term 'idea' is often used interchangeably with 'theme', 'meaning', or 'message'. These terms mean largely the same thing: the points about life and human actions that are shown in the play.

> **REVISION TIP**
> Make sure that any comments you make about methods directly support the point you are making about an idea. Notice how the comments in the table naturally combine points about method and ideas.

Knowledge 3

Knowledge — PLOT

1 Act One

Key idea	How methods are used to show these ideas
Evil influence	Shakespeare chooses to open the play by focusing on the witches in a stormy outdoor setting to suggest their darkness. We see the process by which they trigger Macbeth's ambition. Lady Macbeth's influence over her husband suggests that his disastrous choice to kill Duncan is partly the result of her evil influence too. Her immediate thoughts on the murder are revealed in soliloquy.
Trust and deception	The play opens with a suggestion of Macbeth's trustworthiness and reward for it, but he is soon shown to mistakenly put his trust in the witches. When the Macbeths greet Duncan, the audience knows they are plotting his death. This use of **dramatic irony** encourages them to pity Duncan and see the Macbeths as conniving.

REMEMBER
AO2 is about methods. This means anything that Shakespeare does to present the story, such as what he has the characters do and say, the way a text begins, develops and ends, settings, **dialogue**, and **figurative language**.

LINK
You can find out more about methods on page 7.

Five key lines

1 'to win us to our harm,
The instruments of darkness tell us truths'

Banquo warns Macbeth not to trust the witches' seductive words.

2 'why do I yield to that suggestion,
Whose horrid image doth unfix my hair'

Macbeth wonders why he's giving in to the alarming thought of killing Duncan.

3 'I fear thy nature,
It is too full o'th'milk of human kindness'

Lady Macbeth thinks that her husband is too nice to kill for ambition.

4 'look like th'innocent flower,
But be the serpent under't'

Lady Macbeth advises her husband to appear innocent and keep his evil hidden.

5 'I have no spur
To prick the sides of my intent, but only
Vaulting ambition'

Macbeth realises the only reason he has to kill Duncan is his ambition.

REVISION TIP
You are not marked on the number of quotations you use. References – where you paraphrase parts of the text rather than quote directly – are equally useful.

Use quotations from the extract in the exam paper, but only use ones that are relevant to the question.

Key terms — Make sure you can write a definition for these key terms: contrast, dialogue, dramatic irony, figurative language, genre, method, soliloquy, structure, tragedy

Retrieval 1

Answer the questions below. Cover the answers column with a piece of paper and write down as many answers as you can. Check and repeat.

	Questions	Answers
1	Which two main characters have helped defeat the rebels and invaders?	Macbeth and Banquo
2	What title does Duncan give to Macbeth as a reward?	Thane of Cawdor
3	What do the witches imply about Macbeth's future?	That he will become Thane of Cawdor and, in the future, king
4	How does Macbeth react to the witches' predictions?	He privately wonders how he could become king
5	Who does Duncan say will be the next king?	Malcolm
6	How does Lady Macbeth react to the news of the witches' predictions?	She wants her husband to be king but thinks he lacks the desire to act
7	What does Lady Macbeth think her husband lacks?	One from: The desire to act / The evil that accompanies ambition
8	What does Macbeth initially think about killing Duncan?	He decides against it
9	How does Lady Macbeth influence her husband?	She accuses her husband of being a coward and proposes a plan
10	Name a method Shakespeare uses to reveal Macbeth's thoughts.	Soliloquy
11	What does Macbeth say is his only reason for killing Duncan?	Ambition
12	How does the use of dramatic irony affect the way the audience sees Duncan and the Macbeths?	It encourages the audience to pity Duncan and see the Macbeths as conniving, as we know what's coming
13	Complete the quotation using three words. 'The _____ tell us truths;'	'The <u>instruments of darkness</u> tell us truths;'
14	Complete the quotation. 'look like th' _____ flower, But be the _____ under't.'	'look like th'<u>innocent</u> flower, But be the <u>serpent</u> under't.'
15	Give three elements of Macbeth's tragic journey as seen in Act 1.	He is a powerful character with a fatal flaw, he makes a terrible decision, he suffers as a result

Knowledge   PLOT

2 Act Two

Macbeth's tragic journey

There are two conventional tragic events in this act:

- Macbeth ignores his own concerns about the murder and goes ahead and kills Duncan – he makes a fatal choice that will have serious repercussions.
- Macbeth begins to suffer as a result of his actions – he experiences mental turmoil and is never happy again from this point in the play.

> **REVISION TIP**
>
> As you re-read the plot of each act of the play, look out for key moments in Macbeth's tragic journey. Look for moments where he makes tragic errors and where their consequences emerge.

Key events

Macbeth kills Duncan, having imagined a dagger leading him to Duncan's chamber. After, Macbeth feels remorse. Other characters are suspicious of Macbeth's actions. By the end of the act, Macbeth is about to be crowned king.

Scene 1
- Banquo and Fleance, his son, walk through Macbeth's castle at midnight.
- Banquo says his sleep has been disturbed by sinister thoughts.
- Banquo and Macbeth agree to discuss the witches' predictions at a later point.
- Macbeth claims he has not thought about the witches' predictions.
- On his way to murder Duncan, Macbeth sees a vision of a floating dagger.

Scene 2
- Lady Macbeth waits for Macbeth to return.
- Macbeth murders Duncan. He mistakenly brings, but refuses to return, the daggers.
- Lady Macbeth accuses him of cowardice and returns the daggers herself.

Scene 3
- A castle porter lets in the thane Macduff, who has come to collect the king.
- Duncan's body is discovered, and Lady Macbeth claims to be horrified.
- The king's sons, Malcolm and Donaldbain, are told that Duncan's chamberlains are assumed to be guilty of his murder.
- Macbeth says that, in a rage, he killed the chamberlains, but Macduff isn't convinced by Macbeth's explanation.
- Lady Macbeth faints and is taken away.
- The king's sons, Malcolm and Donaldbain, flee Scotland for safety.

Scene 4
- Macbeth will be crowned as king, but Macduff decides to avoid the ceremony.

> **REMEMBER**
>
> The audience usually knows characters' motivations and secrets, but characters on stage may not. When thinking about method, think about which characters are allowed to know what, and when.

> **REVISION TIP**
>
> Look closely at how initial problems are developed and intensified in the middle acts of the play. Note how Shakespeare complicates the relationships between characters. Make sure you understand what happens and in what order.

Key ideas of Act Two

Writing about the big ideas of the text is the most important aspect of your studies. But you also need to understand *how* these ideas are presented – the methods that Shakespeare uses to show these ideas.

Use the plot of the play to track how the main characters develop. One way to do this is to identify the key moments in a story where they change or make a vital decision. Often these moments are preceded and followed by scenes where the character reflects on their actions.

Tragedy explores the effects of making a terrible error. Notice how many of the ideas and events noted in the table are the result of Macbeth's decision to murder Duncan.

Key idea	How methods are used to show these ideas
Trust and deception	Shakespeare uses dramatic irony to show how Macbeth is now deceiving the other thanes. The audience knows that he is lying to cover up the murder. The dialogue given to Macduff, Malcolm, and Donaldbain also reveals their mistrust of Macbeth.
Warning	The **symbol** of the floating dagger that Macbeth sees acts as a warning – an indication of the bloody journey he is choosing to go on. In tragic terms, it is a warning that he ignores.
Murder and violence	Shakespeare presents Duncan's murder offstage – the audience never sees this, but gory details of blood and daggers create a macabre mood. There is a contrast between Macbeth's unfeeling brutality on the battlefield and his remorseful reaction to killing Duncan, which suggests he still has some moral feelings.
Power	Shakespeare shows how power is gained through violent acts and fear. The murder of a monarch – regicide – is motivated by a desire for power. The decision to kill a king is seen as upsetting the natural order in the world of the play.
Suffering	Macbeth's remorse is immediate. He realises the scale of his actions and says he is alarmed by noises and fears he will never remove the blood from his hands. This symbol recurs in the play.

> **REVISION TIP**
>
> High-quality responses are written fluently and use words precisely. Check you understand the exact meaning of any complex vocabulary. Sometimes, complex vocabulary is required to express the concepts dealt with in the play, but don't use complex vocabulary just for the sake of it.

> **REVISION TIP**
>
> Take note of how character traits and attitudes are established in early acts of the play and then how some are developed or even reversed as the narrative progresses. Track these developments as you revise the plot.

> **REMEMBER**
>
> Thinking about dramatic irony, symbol, and dialogue will naturally lead you to explore the big ideas of a text in a way that writing about something smaller, like alliteration, doesn't.

Knowledge

Knowledge — PLOT

2 Act Two

Five key lines

1 'Or art thou but
A dagger of the mind, a false creation,
Proceeding from the heat-oppressed brain?'

Macbeth wonders if the dagger he sees is a result of the mental turmoil he is experiencing.

2 'Had he not resembled my father as he slept,
I had done't.'

Lady Macbeth offers a reason why she didn't commit the murder, maybe revealing some humanity, but this idea is undermined when she returns the daggers.

3 'What hands are here?
Ha: they pluck out mine eyes.'

Macbeth is alarmed at the blood on his hands as he realises the magnitude of what he has done.

4 'A little water clears us of this deed.'

Lady Macbeth nonchalantly suggests that washing hands will get rid of the blood and any feelings of guilt; later, this proves to be incorrect.

5 'Where we are,
There's daggers in men's smiles'

Donaldbain suggests to Malcolm that Macbeth is the type of person who pretends to be welcoming while planning your death.

REMEMBER

Although many of the play's ideas are conveyed through literal speech, they are supported and reinforced by figurative uses of language. Often, when a memorable metaphor or image is used, its function is to reinforce a key idea.

 **Key terms** Make sure you can write a definition for this key term

symbol

Retrieval 2

Answer the questions below. Cover the answers column with a piece of paper and write down as many answers as you can. Check and repeat.

Questions | Answers

#	Question	Answer
1	What symbolic object does Macbeth see on his way to murder Duncan?	A floating dagger
2	What does Macbeth mistakenly bring with him after he kills Duncan?	The daggers
3	Who is assumed to have killed Duncan?	Duncan's chamberlains
4	Why do the king's sons leave Scotland?	For safety
5	Describe Macduff's feelings about the murder and his attitude towards Macbeth.	He isn't convinced by Macbeth's explanation and avoids Macbeth's crowning
6	Explain one effect of Shakespeare's use of dramatic irony in Act 2.	Shakespeare uses it to show Macbeth is now deceiving the other thanes
7	Give two things that show Macbeth's suffering after the murder of Duncan.	He is alarmed by noises and fears he will never remove the blood from his hands
8	Complete the quotation using three words. 'A little _____ of this deed.'	'A little water clears us of this deed.'
9	Complete the quotation. 'Where we are, There's _____ in men's smiles;'	'Where we are, There's daggers in men's smiles;'
10	Give two events in Macbeth's tragic journey that occur in Act 2.	He ignores concerns and goes ahead with murder, he begins to suffer as a result

Previous questions

Now go back and use these questions to check your knowledge of previous topics.

Questions | Answers

#	Question	Answer
1	What title does Duncan give to Macbeth as a reward?	Thane of Cawdor
2	How does Macbeth react to the witches' predictions?	He privately wonders how he could become king
3	How does Lady Macbeth influence her husband?	She accuses her husband of being a coward and proposes a plan
4	Name a method Shakespeare uses to reveal Macbeth's thoughts.	Soliloquy
5	Give three elements of Macbeth's tragic journey as seen in Act 1.	He is a powerful character with a fatal flaw, he makes a terrible decision, he suffers as a result

Knowledge `PLOT`

3 Act Three

Macbeth's tragic journey

Act 3 shows the continuation of Macbeth's tragic experience:

- He suffers mental anguish and is not content with his new-found power.
- Hecate and the witches continue to plot Macbeth's torture and downfall, and he is unaware of this.
- His terrible decisions are beginning to have consequences. Macduff's visit to England is the beginning of the end for Macbeth.

> **REMEMBER**
> Shakespeare's use of dramatic irony has different effects at different points in the play. As Macbeth's downfall begins, the audience is allowed to see how Macduff's plot against Macbeth develops and how Hecate plans to play with Macbeth. Macbeth doesn't see this, and, for some readers, this creates a sense of pity.

> **REVISION TIP**
> Explore how Shakespeare structures the downfall of Macbeth. Look at which points feelings of suffering and remorse are placed in the sequence of the story, and at which points they are most acute.

Key events

Suspicions grow about Macbeth. He arranges the murders of Banquo and Fleance, but Fleance escapes. Banquo's ghost appears to Macbeth at a banquet and causes him to act irrationally. Macbeth decides to visit the witches again.

Scene 1
- Banquo thinks about the witches' predictions, wondering if Macbeth has killed Duncan.
- Macbeth, now king, invites Banquo to a banquet.
- Macbeth suggests to Banquo that they should discuss Duncan's sons, who are now suspected of their father's murder.
- Macbeth thinks about Banquo, seeing him and his son as a threat to his power.
- Macbeth instructs two murderers to kill Banquo and Fleance.

Scene 2
- Macbeth says to his wife that they aren't fully secure in their reign yet, but doesn't tell her of the plan to kill Banquo and Fleance.

Scene 3
- The murderers kill Banquo, but Fleance escapes.

> **REVISION TIP**
> The middle part of a play usually has lots of plot development that prepares for the end of the play. Track the key moments that intensify the problems that lead to Macbeth's eventual downfall.

> **REMEMBER**
> Macbeth fears Fleance because the witches have said that Banquo's sons will rule Scotland. Macbeth sees Banquo and his son as a threat.

Scene 4

- At the banquet, Macbeth is told that Banquo is dead, but Fleance escaped alive.
- Banquo's ghost appears and is visible to Macbeth only. Macbeth speaks to it.
- Lady Macbeth makes excuses to the guests for her husband's strange behaviour.
- The ghost reappears and Macbeth is alarmed. The banquet ends in disorder.
- Macbeth says he is suspicious of Macduff and will return to see the witches.

Scene 5

- In a deserted place, the witches meet Hecate, queen of witches, who says she will further confuse Macbeth.

Scene 6

- Lennox and another thane discuss their suspicions of Macbeth for both murders.
- Lennox says that Macduff has gone to England to seek Malcolm and England's help to overthrow Macbeth.

> **REVISION TIP**
> Stage and film performances differ in the way they present certain scenes. Some even cut lines or scenes. Try to watch different versions of key scenes and explore the ways in which each version presents the text. However, remember that in your exam it is the words of the original text that are most important!

Key ideas of Act Three

Writing about the big ideas of the text is the most important aspect of your studies. But you also need to understand *how* these ideas are presented – the methods that Shakespeare uses to show these ideas.

Key idea	How methods are used to show these ideas
Trust and deception	Shakespeare uses soliloquy to reveal how both Banquo and Macbeth mistrust each other. The use of dramatic irony allows the audience to see how each man acts towards the other while they conceal their inner thoughts. Macbeth then places his trust in the murderers who ultimately let him down.
Ambition	Banquo's initial soliloquy shows how he has ambitions for his son. The witches' predictions have awoken ambitions in both men, although Macbeth alone acts upon these desires. Shakespeare shows how unchecked ambition leads to terrible outcomes and mental turmoil.
Violence and power	Shakespeare presents the second murder in the play as one motivated by a desire to maintain power. The audience sees how Macbeth now has no doubts about the act of murder: his dialogue and attitude contrast with his feelings about Duncan's murder. Power is shown to be more important than loyalty and friendship for Macbeth.

> **REVISION TIP**
> When you explore plot, think how some events act as a contrast to others and how certain events are echoed in other parts of the play. In doing so, you are beginning to see how Shakespeare uses structural ideas to create meanings.

> **REVISION TIP**
> Ask a partner to test your knowledge of a single main idea. For example, you might be asked to recall the main events of the play that link to ideas of evil. Try to give as much detail as possible from across the whole play rather than just a small section of it.

Knowledge

 # Knowledge PLOT

3 Act Three

Key idea	How methods are used to show these ideas
Evil and the supernatural	Macbeth's lack of moral feeling about murder, especially that of young Fleance, suggests a sense of evil. Banquo's ghost acts as a symbol of Macbeth's guilt, suggesting that it is impossible to kill without paying for it in some way. Dramatic irony allows the audience to see how Hecate and the witches are playing with Macbeth: the audience can see how blind Macbeth is to his growing tragedy.
Disorder	The banquet is a symbol of power and order, but Macbeth's odd behaviour and the disarray in which the banquet ends symbolises Macbeth's chaotic reign.

REMEMBER
As you become more confident with the ideas of the text, you will notice that many of them are interlinked. For example, Macbeth's ambitions are connected with power and, in following these ambitions, he performs evil acts. Be comfortable with the way that many of the ideas are connected.

Five key lines

1 'I fear
Thou played'st most foully for't'

Banquo expresses his suspicions about Macbeth and how he came to power.

2 'Our fears in Banquo
Stick deep, and in his royalty of nature
Reigns that which would be fear'd.'

Macbeth expresses his mistrust of Banquo, whose nobility (in addition to the witches' predictions about his sons) are a threat to Macbeth's future as king.

REVISION TIP
If you decide to learn quotations, spend time experimenting with different methods. Some students find that repeating them aloud helps best.

3 'We have scorch'd the snake, not kill'd it'

Macbeth tells his wife that they have temporarily stopped any threats to their rule, but aren't fully safe. He is worried about the future, and especially about Fleance.

4 'O, full of scorpions is my mind, dear wife!'

Macbeth tells his wife of his mental turmoil.

5 'I am in blood
Stepp'd in so far that should I wade no more,
Returning were as tedious as go o'er.'

Macbeth says that he has spilt so much of Duncan's blood that murdering again would make little difference.

Retrieval

Answer the questions below. Cover the answers column with a piece of paper and write down as many answers as you can. Check and repeat.

Questions | Answers

1. How does Banquo feel about Macbeth at the start of Act 3? — He wonders if Macbeth has killed Duncan
2. Macbeth plans to kill Banquo with his own hands. True or false? — False. He instructs two murderers to kill Banquo (and Fleance)
3. What does Macbeth tell his wife of the plot to kill Banquo and Fleance? — Nothing
4. Where does Macduff go to and why? — To England to seek Malcolm and England's help to overthrow Macbeth
5. Explain the function of dramatic irony in Macbeth and Banquo's dialogue. — It allows the audience to see how each man acts towards the other while they conceal their inner thoughts
6. What does Banquo's ghost symbolise? — Macbeth's guilt
7. How does Macbeth's feelings about the upcoming murders contrast with his feelings about Duncan's murder? — Macbeth now has no doubts about the act of murder
8. Complete the quotation using three words. 'We have _____, not kill'd it;' — 'We have scorch'd the snake, not kill'd it;'
9. Complete the quotation using three words. 'O, _____ is my mind, dear wife!' — 'O, full of scorpions is my mind, dear wife!'
10. Give two examples of tragic aspects in Act 3. — Two from: Macbeth suffers mental anguish / the witches continue to plot his fall / we see the consequence of his actions

Previous questions

Now go back and use these questions to check your knowledge of previous topics.

Questions | Answers

1. Which two main characters have helped defeat the rebels and invaders? — Macbeth and Banquo
2. What does Lady Macbeth think her husband lacks? — One from: The desire to act / The evil that accompanies ambition
3. Give two events in Macbeth's tragic journey that occur in Act 2. — He ignores concerns and goes ahead with murder, he begins to suffer as a result
4. Who is assumed to have killed Duncan? — Duncan's chamberlains
5. Why do the king's sons leave Scotland? — For safety

Knowledge PLOT

4 Act Four

Macbeth's tragic journey

When audiences watch a tragedy, they are aware that it will end with the death of the main character. The main interest therefore lies in how the tragedy comes about, rather than the inevitable end. When you write about tragedy, focus on the way it is structured and how each decision made by Macbeth is a staging post in his downfall.

Further developments in Macbeth's gradual downfall happen in Act 4:

- He continues to make the mistake of trusting the witches, even though he knows they are untrustworthy.
- His decision to kill Macduff's family will lead directly to Macbeth's own death at the end of the play.
- Characters who Macbeth has harmed – Malcolm and Macduff – are set up as revengers.

REMEMBER

Although it's interesting to try to identify one key error made by a tragic character, very often it's a series of bad choices that leads to their downfall. For Macbeth, sometimes he is aware that his decisions are poor but still goes ahead. At other times he is unaware that the decisions and actions he takes will bring further problems.

Key events

Macbeth revisits the witches, who give him further predictions. He is both reassured and troubled by these. He arranges the murders of Macduff's family as a result of one of these predictions. In England, Macduff and Malcolm meet and discuss overthrowing Macbeth. Macduff learns that his family have been killed.

Scene 1

- In a deserted place, the witches chant spells around a cauldron and Hecate (queen of witches) praises their work.
- Macbeth asks the witches what the future holds. They show him a series of apparitions who speak to him.
- Macbeth is told to beware of Macduff.
- He is told that 'none of woman born' will harm him.
- He is told he will be safe until Birnam Wood comes to Dunsinane Hill.
- Along with Banquo's ghost, Macbeth is shown a procession of eight kings that imply Banquo's sons will reign for a long time in Scotland.
- Lennox tells Macbeth that Macduff has left for England. Macbeth decides to send murderers to kill Macduff's wife and children.

Scene 2

- Lady Macduff asks Ross, another thane, why her husband has left. She feels betrayed.
- A messenger warns Lady Macduff to flee, but murderers arrive and kill the whole family.

REVISION TIP

Take note of settings and locations where plot events occur. Shakespeare contrasts the events that take place in powerful royal locations with the plot events that occur in the strange world of the witches.

REMEMBER

The murders in the play are shown in different ways and have different functions. For example, Duncan's murder takes place offstage and shows the extent of Macbeth's ambitions and the magnitude of his crimes. The brutal death of the Macduffs prompts Macduff's revenge.

Scene 3

- In England, Malcolm and Macduff speak and Malcolm says he doesn't trust Macduff.
- Malcolm talks about his own weaknesses as a way of testing Macduff.
- Ross arrives and tells Macduff that his family has been murdered.
- Macduff promises to seek revenge.

> **REVISION TIP**
>
> When re-reading the play, don't skip Act 4 Scene 3. It reveals much about the character of Malcolm. Take note of how it shows his attitudes towards kingship in comparison to Macbeth's.

Key ideas of Act Four

Writing about the big ideas of the text is the most important aspect of your studies. But you also need to understand *how* these ideas are presented – the methods that Shakespeare uses to show these ideas.

Key idea	How methods are used to show these ideas
Trust and deception	Shakespeare shows how Macbeth mistakenly decides to trust the witches' words. Their misleading language gives him optimism but also concerns about the future. Dramatic irony allows the audience to realise that the witches are playing with him.
The supernatural	Shakespeare uses aspects of setting to suggest things about the witches. The deserted location, thunder, and ingredients referred to in their dialogue suggest unsettling and disturbing qualities, which alert the audience to their evil and Macbeth's foolishness in trusting them.
Power	Although Macbeth is a powerful king, he puts himself in the power of the witches' words. Shakespeare builds the scene to a **climax** where Macbeth is left angry and dismayed by what he has been shown by the witches.
Evil	Shakespeare contrasts the innocent domestic world of the Macduffs with the cruel, evil actions of Macbeth's murderers. This part of the play shows how far Macbeth has changed – these evil acts are motivated by punishment rather than political power. The murders act as a **turning point** in the play, as it leads to Macduff killing Macbeth.
Kingship	Shakespeare explores kingship – the manner in which a king rules – by contrasting Macbeth's terrible reign and Malcolm's more cautious and thoughtful attitudes.

> **REVISION TIP**
>
> Look for moments in a plot where climaxes and turning points occur. These high points in a story often reveal key things about characters and situations and set up the end of the story.

> **REMEMBER**
>
> Contrast is a powerful method to reveal ideas and can be very useful to write about. For instance, in Act 4, you might explore how Macbeth's association with the chaotic world of the witches contrasts with Malcolm's measured and thoughtful English court, and what this implies about the two men's attitudes towards power.

Knowledge

Knowledge — PLOT

4 Act Four

Five key lines

1 'Something wicked this way comes'

The witches announce the entrance of Macbeth and comment on his inherent evil.

2 'Infected be the air whereon they ride,
And damn'd all those that trust them.'

Macbeth curses the witches and notes that those who trust them are doomed.

3 'Not in the legions
Of horrid hell can come a devil more damn'd In evils'

Macduff identifies the scale of Macbeth's evil and links him to evil beings.

4 'let grief
Convert to anger.
Blunt not the heart, enrage it'

Malcolm advises Macduff to use the murder of his family as motivation to kill Macbeth.

5 'Macbeth Is ripe for shaking, and the powers above
Put on their instruments.'

Malcolm says that Macbeth deserves to be attacked and that God is on their side.

> **REVISION TIP**
> Don't spend lots of time trying to learn quotations. Focus on remembering the big ideas and character details.
>
> If you do learn quotations, choose short, memorable ones that can be used in a variety of questions. You will not be penalised for slightly incorrect quotations.

> **REVISION TIP**
> To revise the full narrative of the play, you could map out the five acts in terms of where the major events and turning points occur. Use the plot summaries in this book to help you identify them. Then explore how these events are linked and how one event leads to another. You might consider which is the most significant event in the whole play in terms of Macbeth's downfall.

Key terms — Make sure you can write a definition for these key terms: climax · turning point

Retrieval

4

Answer the questions below. Cover the answers column with a piece of paper and write down as many answers as you can. Check and repeat.

Questions	Answers
1. Name three things the apparitions tell Macbeth.	Beware of Macduff; 'None of woman born' will harm him; He will be safe until Birnam Wood comes to Dunsinane Hill
2. What other supernatural being appears alongside the eight kings?	Banquo's ghost
3. What does the procession of eight kings imply to Macbeth?	Banquo's sons will reign for a long time in Scotland
4. How does Lady Macduff feel about her husband's departure?	She feels betrayed
5. Why does Malcolm talk about his weaknesses to Macduff?	To test Macduff
6. Give one example of how the tragic consequences of Macbeth's actions are shown in Act 4.	One from: He suffers mental anguish and is not content with his new-found power / Macduff's visit to England is the beginning of the end for Macbeth
7. How does Shakespeare use setting to suggest the witches' qualities?	The deserted location, thunder, and ingredients referred to suggest unsettling and disturbing qualities, which alert the audience to their evil
8. What does kingship mean, and what is suggested about Malcolm's future reign?	The manner in which a king rules; Malcolm will be more cautious and thoughtful
9. Complete the quotation. 'Infected be the air whereon they ride, And _____ all those that _____ them'	'Infected be the air whereon they ride, And <u>damn'd</u> all those that <u>trust</u> them.'
10. Complete the quotation using three words. 'Not in the legions Of horrid hell can come a _____ In evils'	'Not in the legions Of horrid hell can come a <u>devil more damn'd</u> In evils'

Previous questions

Now go back and use these questions to check your knowledge of previous topics.

Questions	Answers
1. Who does Duncan say will be the next king?	Malcolm
2. Why do the king's sons leave Scotland?	For safety
3. How does Banquo feel about Macbeth at the start of Act 3?	He wonders if Macbeth has killed Duncan

Knowledge PLOT

5 Act Five

Macbeth's tragic journey

Tragedy not only shows the downfall and death of a character, it also contains moments where the character is made to face the mess that they have created. Macbeth is shown reflecting on the pointlessness of life and his loss of honour. This type of scene is conventional in tragedy. Being made to face the results of your actions prior to your death is part of typical tragic suffering.

The end of the play uses conventional aspects of tragedy:

- Macbeth comes to realise how his mistakes have made his life unhappy and pointless.
- Macbeth's death brings about an end to the misery and cruelty he has created.
- Malcolm's new reign suggests that better times lie ahead.

REMEMBER

The final words in a play are usually highly significant, as is which character speaks them. Shakespeare gives the final words of the play to Malcolm, suggesting that a new and more thoughtful king is about to rule and a new and more balanced order will be established.

Key events

Lady Macbeth sleepwalks and seems to be reliving Duncan's murder. She soon kills herself, and Macbeth reflects on life. Soldiers gather outside Macbeth's castle, and it appears the witches' prediction about Birnam Wood is coming true. Macduff kills Macbeth, and Malcolm is proclaimed king.

Scene 1
- A visiting Doctor and Gentlewoman witness Lady Macbeth's sleepwalking. Lady Macbeth enters, sleepwalking. She talks, referencing previous murders.
- Lady Macbeth tries to wash imaginary blood from her hands, and appears to have lost her sanity.

Scene 2
- The Scottish and English armies meet outside Macbeth's castle.

Scene 3
- Macbeth thinks he cannot be harmed and puts on his armour.
- Macbeth orders the Doctor to cure Lady Macbeth.

Scene 4
- Outside the castle, the soldiers cut down trees to camouflage themselves as they approach the castle, and this suggests Birnam Wood comes to Dunsinane.

REVISION TIP

The endings of stories often contain a lot of action and plot events. Note how previous problems and conflicts are brought to an end and look for moments that suggest better times lie ahead.

Scene 5
- Lady Macbeth dies (later confirmed as suicide in Malcolm's final speech).
- Macbeth reflects on the meaninglessness of life, but promises to fight on, saying he can't be harmed by one 'born of woman'.

Scene 6
- Malcolm instructs Siward and Macduff to attack the castle.

Scene 7
- Macbeth kills Young Siward. Malcolm and Siward's father enter the castle.

Scene 8
- Macbeth discovers Macduff was born by caesarean section, so not 'of woman born' in the normal way, and is killed by him.

Scene 9
- Macduff enters with Macbeth's decapitated head.
- Macduff proclaims Malcolm the new King of Scotland.
- Malcolm offers the thanes greater powers and invites them to see him crowned.

> **REVISION TIP**
> Take careful note of the very last scene of the play, and especially Malcolm's final words. Make sure you explore them and what they show about Malcolm's rule.

Key ideas of Act Five

Writing about the big ideas of the text is the most important aspect of your studies. But you also need to understand *how* these ideas are presented – the methods that Shakespeare uses to show these ideas.

Key idea	How methods are used to show these ideas
Suffering	Shakespeare uses Lady Macbeth's **character arc** to show how terrible actions can lead to suffering. Her mental turmoil and death contrast with her power at the start of the play, suggesting that evil behaviour results in punishment.
Trust and deception	Shakespeare shows the ultimate result of Macbeth mistakenly trusting the witches' words – it leads to his death in the **resolution** of the play. His own selfish ambitions have led him to be deceived.
Death and power	Shakespeare presents a brutal world where violence and death are the only means to get power. The murder of Macbeth at the end of the play is a **narrative echo** of Duncan's murder in Act 2, except Macbeth's demise seems more morally justified.

> **REVISION TIP**
> The final section of a text often makes a significant contribution to the ideas of a play. Explore how key moments, such as Macbeth's death, help to make a point about the dangers of ambition.

> **REVISION TIP**
> Look for moments in the story's ending where ideas or events are revisited. These echoes and contrasts help to make meanings emerge and show differences in characters' attitudes.

Knowledge 19

Knowledge — PLOT

5 Act Five

Key idea	How methods are used to show these ideas
Punishment	The resolution of the play shows the Macbeths receiving their comeuppance for their terrible actions. Shakespeare uses this part of the play to reinforce a moral message, that selfish, disruptive acts must be paid for.
Kingship	The actions of Malcolm at the resolution are an attempt to heal Scotland: he wants to share more power with the thanes and looks for their support. Shakespeare echoes the noble rule of Duncan here and contrasts Malcolm's manner with Macbeth's selfish reign.

REMEMBER
Some characters are given definite endings in the play, and this helps to make moral points. For instance, the deaths of the Macbeths can be seen as suitable punishment for their actions. Other characters have less of a definite ending. For instance, the witches 'disappear' from the story, which may indicate how true evil can avoid punishment.

Five key lines

1 'What, will these hands ne'er be clean?'
Lady Macbeth talks in her sleep about the imagined blood on her hands.

2 'Life's but a walking shadow, a poor player'
Macbeth compares life to an insubstantial shadow and a bad actor.

3 'It is a tale
Told by an idiot, full of sound and fury
Signifying nothing.'
Macbeth compares life to a ridiculous, noisy story that means nothing.

4 'I bear a charmed life which must not yield
To one of woman born.'
Macbeth confidently assumes that no one can kill him.

5 'this dead butcher and his fiend-like queen'
Malcolm's final assessment of the murderous, evil Macbeths.

REVISION TIP
Make notes exploring how figurative language is used to relay misery. Notice where tragedy is expressed in creative language at the darkest moments in the play.

Key terms
Make sure you can write a definition for these key terms: character arc, narrative echo, resolution

Retrieval

5

Answer the questions below. Cover the answers column with a piece of paper and write down as many answers as you can. Check and repeat.

Questions | Answers

#	Questions	Answers
1	What does Lady Macbeth talk about and do when she sleepwalks?	She refers to the previous murders and tries to wash her hands of blood
2	How does the forest come to the castle?	The soldiers cut down trees to camouflage themselves as they approach
3	What is Macbeth's reaction to his wife's death and his own situation?	He reflects on the meaninglessness of life but promises to fight on
4	Who does Macbeth kill?	Young Siward
5	What does Macduff do after he kills Macbeth?	Cuts his head off (decapitates him)
6	What moral message emerges from the deaths of the Macbeths?	That selfish, disruptive acts must be paid for
7	What suggests that Malcolm will be a good, unselfish king?	He wants to share more power with the thanes and looks for their support
8	Give an example of an event from Act 5 that echoes an event from Act 2.	Macbeth's death echoes that of Duncan's
9	Complete the quotation using three words. 'Life's but a _____, a _____ player'	'Life's but a <u>walking shadow</u>, a <u>poor</u> player'
10	Complete the quotation using five words. 'It is a tale Told by an _____, full of _____ _____ nothing.'	'It is a tale Told by an <u>idiot</u>, full of <u>sound and fury</u> <u>Signifying</u> nothing.'
11	Give three tragic events that occur in Act 5.	Macbeth realises his mistakes have made his life unhappy and pointless; His death ends the misery and cruelty he created; Malcolm's reign suggests better times lie ahead

Previous questions

Now go back and use these questions to check your knowledge of previous topics.

Questions | Answers

#	Questions	Answers
1	What symbolic object does Macbeth see on his way to murder Duncan?	A floating dagger
2	What does Banquo's ghost symbolise?	Macbeth's guilt

# Knowledge METHODS

6 Writer's methods

What are writer's methods?

'Methods' (AO2) refers to the ways a writer presents their ideas: anything they choose to do to show the story, characters, and ideas. This means the larger structural methods such as the big events of the text, their order, and how characters are used in the story. It also means the smaller aspects of text such as metaphor and language choices.

> **LINK**
> You can read more examples of how to refer to methods in the sample answers on pages 27–28.

> **REMEMBER**
> Beginning a sentence with 'Shakespeare decides to…' or 'Shakespeare uses…' alerts the examiner that you are focusing on an aspect of method. It shows that you are aware the writer has deliberately chosen to present ideas in a certain way.

> **REVISION TIP**
> The most important thing to focus on in an exam response is ideas and meanings. Lead with your ideas, and only comment on methods that are relevant to those ideas.

Dramatic structure and focus

Dramatic structure means the order of events in the play. It means how **conflicts** and problems are introduced, how they develop, and what happens in the resolution of the play. Shakespeare deliberately chooses the order in which **key events** are shown to the audience, and this influences how the audience interprets those ideas.

Shakespeare chooses what to focus the audience's attention upon. He decides how much stage time to give to certain events, and which events to minimise or show offstage. For example, he focuses our attention on Macbeth's feelings prior to killing Duncan – rather than the actual murder – which draws attention to the character's conflicted feelings and explores ideas about morality and ambition.

Here are three more examples of structural choices, and how you can write about their effect upon meaning and ideas.

> **REVISION TIP**
> Use structural terms when you are referring to key parts of the story. Practise using terms such as 'climax', 'establish', and 'resolution' in your writing.

> **REMEMBER**
> It is often best to focus on structural methods, as they are the most significant ways in which meanings are created. Be careful not to simply focus on individual words all of the time.

Structural choice	Effect upon meaning and ideas
Shakespeare chooses to open the play with the witches' scene (Act 1 Scene 1).	The audience is alerted to the importance of the supernatural straight away. By opening the play with the witches, Shakespeare **establishes** their potential influence over events: by showing them planning to meet Macbeth before he is introduced on stage, it suggests that they have some control and authority in the world of the text.

Structural choice	Effect upon meaning and ideas
Shakespeare decides to have Fleance escape from the murderers who kill his father (Act 3 Scene 3).	Fleance's survival keeps alive the witches' prophecy about Banquo's sons. This increases the **tension** in the play – it intensifies Macbeth's suffering when he learns of Fleance's escape in the next scene and is another stage in the ramping up of Macbeth's tragic journey.
Shakespeare decides to reveal the truth of Macduff's caesarean birth towards the end of the play (Act 5 Scene 8).	This **revelation** clears up the witches' cryptic prophecy from Act 4 Scene 1 and suggests to Macbeth that he is likely to die soon in the climax of the play. It also confirms to him (and the audience) that he has been a fool to put his trust in the witches' words.

Contrast

Writers often present characters and situations with contrasting values, actions, and ideas. Doing so brings closer attention to ideas about human conduct. Here are three examples:

Banquo's cautious reaction to the witches **Contrasts with** Macbeth's willingness to believe the witches

This shows how humans are more likely to be tempted when they stand to directly benefit from something. In a basic way, it also suggests that Banquo is a 'good' character and Macbeth 'bad'.

Lady Macbeth's assertiveness at the beginning of the play **Contrasts with** Lady Macbeth's breakdown at the end of the play

This suggests that her supposed dominance may have been an act, and how the lure of power can lead people to terrible outcomes, which they bring upon themselves.

Macbeth's terrible reign **Contrasts with** Malcolm's more thoughtful approach to kingship

This suggests that selfish and cruel approaches to kingship are doomed to failure and more inclusive and thoughtful ones are preferable.

Knowledge

Knowledge — METHODS

6 Writer's methods

Tragic structure

Shakespeare uses the conventions of the tragedy genre to present the play. These events help meanings about life, morality, and other big ideas to emerge.

> **LINK**
> Look at pages 2, 6, 10, 14 and 18 to remind yourself of the stages of Macbeth's tragic journey.

Tragic convention	Link to ideas and meanings
Macbeth is a respected character with a fatal flaw.	Shakespeare shows Macbeth as a loyal and brave general at the opening of the play. His ambition is encouraged by the witches and his wife. This suggests that even outwardly moral characters can be tempted in certain circumstances and allow their base nature to emerge.
Macbeth makes a terrible decision, even though he knows it's wrong.	Shakespeare shows Macbeth wrestling with his conscience – he understands the dangers of killing Duncan. Banquo reminds him not to trust the witches. Choosing to ignore these warnings suggests that his ambition outweighs his moral scruples. It shows how a lust for power causes people to act in terrible ways.
Macbeth suffers the consequences of his terrible decision.	Shakespeare uses 'dialogue', 'soliloquy', and 'key events' to reveal Macbeth's turmoil and mental anguish. This shows how it's impossible to commit a terrible act without it causing problems for yourself.
Macbeth comes to realise the significance of his decision.	Shakespeare uses soliloquy at the end of the play to show how Macbeth realises that he is isolated and emotionless. This suggests that part of suffering is coming to terms with what you have done.
Macbeth dies as a result of his choices.	Shakespeare uses Macbeth's death in the resolution of the play to show that punishment is inescapable for terrible acts. It reinforces a moral idea – that those who go against the natural order won't get away with it.

'Using' characters

One very important method is how a writer 'uses' characters to reveal ideas and meanings. This means deciding:

- what a character does and says
- the key decisions they make in the story
- how they conduct themselves with other characters
- what they are like at the start of the story
- where they are by the end of the story.

The 'journey' of a character in a play (sometimes called the 'character arc') helps big ideas emerge.

> **REVISION TIP**
> Try mapping out which characters live and die by the end of the play, and the key decisions they (or others) make that influence their position by the end.

> **LINK**
> You can find out more about individual character journeys on pages 30–55.

Dramatic irony

This method refers to the different levels of understanding between the audience and a character(s) on stage. When the audience knows more than a character, it informs the way you perceive the situations shown on stage.

Example	Effect created
Lady Macbeth's gracious attitude to Duncan even though she is planning his murder (Act 1 Scene 6)	This shows Lady Macbeth's conniving nature and introduces ideas about appearance and reality. It also increases sympathy and pity for Duncan.
The Macbeths pretending to be innocent when Duncan's body is discovered (Act 2 Scene 3)	This shows how terrible actions lead to further lies and increase the unsympathetic view of the Macbeths.
The thanes' inability to see Banquo's ghost (Act 3 Scene 4)	The audience is aware of what Macbeth seems to be seeing, but the thanes interpret it as a sign of Macbeth's loss of sanity. The audience can see both Macbeth's torment and also how the thanes perceive his odd behaviour.

Speech

In drama, the speech and actions of the character do the telling. The words said by the characters and the way they say them, give you a clue to their personalities and situation. Dialogue can be described in various ways, for example, aggressive dialogue or conspiratorial dialogue.

Example	Effect created
Macbeth's **aside** when presented with the title Thane of Cawdor (Act 1 Scene 3)	This comment reveals his internal thoughts about potentially becoming king. It also shows he is willing to trust the witches and wants to keep his thoughts a secret from Banquo.
Lady Macbeth's **soliloquy** upon reading of her husband's meeting with the witches (Act 1 Scene 5)	This solo speech is the first introduction of Lady Macbeth in the play, and it immediately shows her determination for her husband to be king. It also helps the audience to see her view of Macbeth as being too kindly.
Lady Macbeth's disjointed speech (Act 5 Scene 1)	This reveals her tragic torment that the Macbeths' crimes bring upon her. It reinforces the moral message that terrible acts result in terrible punishment.

> **REMEMBER**
> Speech presented as a soliloquy or an aside is a way to tell you directly what the character is thinking. Look carefully at what they wish to keep hidden from others.

> **REVISION TIP**
> Take careful note of stage directions. Sometimes, they tell you how speech is being delivered, for example, when it is an aside. At other times, you will need to use stage directions to work out who is on stage.

Knowledge — METHODS

6 Writer's methods

Figurative language and imagery

Figurative language refers to figures of speech, such as metaphor. **Imagery** refers to vivid description that appeals to the senses. In *Macbeth*, these smaller aspects of method are often there for descriptive purposes rather than any way to present deep ideas, but there can be instances where it is useful to explore these methods.

Example	Effect created
Imagery: 'The raven himself is hoarse' (Lady Macbeth, Act 1 Scene 5)	The dark imagery in this speech underlines the evil nature of what is being planned and suggests a link between the powers of darkness and Lady Macbeth.
Metaphor: 'We have scorch'd the snake' (Macbeth, Act 3 Scene 2)	This presents threats to power as a snake, suggesting that such threats are dangerous and hard to control.
Metaphor: 'Out, out, brief candle' (Macbeth, Act 5 Scene 5)	This metaphor shows the futility Macbeth experiences by the end of the play and shows where his tragic errors have led him.

> **REMEMBER**
> It can sometimes be hard to decide exactly which type of figurative language is being used – metaphor, **personification**, or imagery. Remember that the important part is what you have to say about it. If in doubt, the term 'figurative language' covers all of these types of techniques.

Word choices

Sometimes, individual word choices can lead to telling points about characters and ideas. It is often the case that such words have a figurative quality.

Example	Effect created
'What cannot you and I perform upon / Th'unguarded Duncan?' (Lady Macbeth, Act 1 Scene 7)	The word 'perform' indicates some sort of relish and conscious action, suggesting that Lady Macbeth will enjoy having power over the dying Duncan.
'I am in blood Stepp'd in so far' (Macbeth, Act 3 Scene 5)	The reference to blood refers to the murders committed and brings to mind the human cost of Macbeth's actions.

> **REVISION TIP**
> If you choose to write about words, you don't need to identify word classes (verb, adverb, etc.).

Example	Effect created
'Out, damned spot!' (Lady Macbeth, Act 5 Scene 1)	The word 'damned' has religious **connotations** and suggests that the character suspects she may go to hell for her actions.

Writing about methods

Sample answer 1: not a strong answer

Here is an extract from a student response, with the examiner's annotations and final comments. They are writing about Macbeth's speech in Act 1 Scene 3, from: 'Two truths are told…' to 'But what is not.' It receives less than half marks.

> Explore how Shakespeare presents Macbeth's attitude towards murder.
>
> [30 marks]
> AO4 [4 marks]

In this speech, Macbeth says that the 'soliciting' is 'supernatural'. This has connotations of the witches as they are supernatural. It shows that he is thinking about the witches and knows that they know the future. ❶ The adjective ❷ 'unfix' in 'unfix my hair' shows that his hair is standing on end, which would shock the reader, and if the reader pictures his hair standing on end, then it would show them what he is thinking and stick in their mind. ❸

❶ Just defining a word here and making a simple point

❷ No need to identify a word class – and this one has been identified incorrectly.

❸ A very general point rather than anything insightful

Examiner's comments

This is a simple response that says nothing about ideas. It does identify a method – words – but makes a very general point. There is little sense of the writer at work.

REVISION TIP

Make sure you write about methods that are relevant to the point you are making. Start by deciding what point you wish to make about an idea and then ask yourself: 'What methods has the writer used to convey this idea?'

REMEMBER

The most important parts of your answer are the points you make about ideas and characters. How those points are conveyed – the methods used – is of secondary importance.

Knowledge

Knowledge **METHODS**

6 Writer's methods

Sample answer 2: a strong answer

Here is an extract from a student response to this question, with the examiner's annotations and final comments. They are writing about Macbeth's speech in Act 1 Scene 3, from: 'Two truths are told…' to 'But what is not.' It receives high marks.

> Explore how Shakespeare presents Macbeth's attitude towards murder.
>
> **[30 marks]**
> **AO4 [4 marks]**

❶ Identifies a structural method and ties it to meaning →

Shakespeare uses this aside to identify Macbeth's conflicted attitude about Duncan's murder. ❶ The contrast between the 'happy prologues' and the image of his unfixed hair suggests this conflict ❷ and gets to the heart of his uncertainty at this point in the play: he is caught in a tragic dilemma between ambition and consequence. ❸

← **❷ Shows how methods are used to create meaning**

❸ Makes a thoughtful point about a key idea →

Examiner's comments

This response directly addresses the question about Macbeth's attitude and makes insightful points about meanings and ideas. Methods are clearly identified. The student clearly understands how Shakespeare presents ideas.

REVISION TIP

Use Shakespeare's name in your work – it shows an examiner that you are focusing on how a text is being constructed and signals that you are making a point about method.

REMEMBER

Do not spend lots of time analysing methods for the sake of it. Instead, identify a relevant method and use it as a way to make a point about ideas or characters. You can see how to do this in Sample answer 2.

Key terms — Make sure you can write a definition for these key terms

| aside | conflict | connotation | establish | imagery |
| key event | personification | revelation | soliloquy | tension |

6 Writer's methods

Retrieval

6

Answer the questions below. Cover the answers column with a piece of paper and write down as many answers as you can. Check and repeat.

Questions | Answers

#	Question	Answer
1	Writing about methods is the most important aspect of a response. True or false?	False
2	Give a basic definition of dramatic structure.	The order of events in the play
3	Explain what a revelation is using an example from *Macbeth*.	When the author reveals the truth of a situation, such as Macduff's caesarean birth
4	The best method to write about is individual words. True or false?	False
5	Give a moral message that emerges from Macbeth's death at the end of the play.	Those who go against the natural order won't get away with it
6	Explain what 'using characters' means.	How a writer reveals ideas and meanings through their decisions about what a character will do, say, and experience
7	Give an example of the use of contrast in the play and the effect created.	One from: Banquo and Macbeth's reactions to the witches / Lady Macbeth at the start and end of the play / Macbeth and Malcolm's kingship
8	Give an example of an aside used in the play and the effect created.	Macbeth's aside when presented with the title Thane of Cawdor (Act 1 Scene 3). Reveals internal thoughts about potentially becoming king, shows Macbeth is willing to trust the witches and wants to keep his thoughts a secret from Banquo
9	'We have scorch'd the snake' Explain what technique is being used here and what it means.	This metaphor presents threats to power as a snake, suggesting that such threats are dangerous and hard to control
10	'Out, out, brief candle' Explain what technique is being used here and what it means.	This metaphor underlines the futility Macbeth experiences by the end of the play and shows where his tragic errors have led him

Previous questions

Now go back and use these questions to check your knowledge of previous topics.

Questions | Answers

#	Question	Answer
1	Macbeth plans to kill Banquo with his own hands. True or false?	False. He instructs two murderers to kill Banquo (and Fleance)
2	What is Macbeth's reaction to his wife's death and his own situation?	He reflects on the meaninglessness of life, but promises to fight on
3	What does Macbeth tell his wife of the plot to kill Banquo and Fleance?	Nothing

Knowledge

CHARACTERS

7 Macbeth

Key ideas of Macbeth's journey

- Rampant ambition leads to terrible situations.
- Power corrupts people.
- People listen to what they want to hear.
- Terrible acts cause a loss of morality and feelings.
- A lust for power destroys relationships.
- Transgressors cannot escape punishment.

> **REVISION TIP**
>
> When revising characters, begin by looking at the major events they are involved in – the key moments. This will help you think about the structural journey of characters and what ideas emerge from their actions.

Key events of Macbeth's journey

① A brave, loyal, and aggressive general who defends Duncan
'he unseam'd him from the nave to th'chaps' (said by the Captain)
— Shakespeare establishes Macbeth as a 'good' character, which contrasts with later actions.

② Witches suggest he will become Thane of Cawdor and king.
'why do I yield to that suggestion,
Whose horrid image doth unfix my hair'
— A turning point in the story, showing how rampant ambition can cause good men to act immorally

③ He is unsure about killing Duncan, but his wife persuades him.
'only
Vaulting ambition which o'erleaps itself'
— Shows the dominance of his wife, which contrasts with her later lack of involvement

④ He kills Duncan, seeing a dagger on the way to his chamber.
'A dagger of the mind'
— A warning that Macbeth ignores on his tragic journey

⑤ He immediately feels guilt at the crime.
'Will all great Neptune's ocean wash this blood
Clean from my hand?'
— The beginning of his suffering and the tragic consequences of his actions

⑥ He becomes king, rules by fear, plotting deaths of Banquo and Fleance.
'For Banquo's issue have I fil'd my mind;'
— The point where he becomes a tyrant and loses more of his humanity

⑦ He is haunted by Banquo's ghost and the banquet ends in chaos.
'broke the good meeting
With most admir'd disorder.'
— Both events symbolise his guilt and the chaos of his reign.

30   7 Macbeth

⑧ **Witches suggest he will be safe but Banquo's children will reign.**
'damn'd all those that trust them'

Another mistake on his tragic journey – he chooses what he wants to hear.

⑨ **He arranges the death of the Macduff family.**
'give to th'edge o'th'sword His wife, his babes'

The lowest point in his loss of morality

⑩ **His wife kills herself and he reacts without emotion.**
'I have supp'd full with horrors'

A key part of his tragic experience – his actions have made him emotionless, and he realises the terrible man he has become.

⑪ **Learns about Macduff's birth and realises the witches have played him.**
'be these juggling fiends no more believ'd'

A key event, where he comes to terms with his error of judgement

⑫ **He is killed and Malcolm takes over.**
'this dead butcher and his fiend-like queen' (said by Malcolm)

The end of his tragic journey, where his reign has ended and problems are resolved.

Key passages for Macbeth

This takes place in Act 1 Scene 7 where Macbeth has been debating killing Duncan.

Macbeth		I have no spur To prick the sides of my intent, but only Vaulting ambition, which o'erleaps itself And falls on th'other— ❶
	5	*Enter Lady Macbeth.*
Macbeth		How now! What news?
Lady Macbeth		He has almost supp'd. Why have you left the chamber?
Macbeth		Hath he ask'd for me?
Lady Macbeth		Know you not, he has? ❷
Macbeth	10	We will proceed no further in this business. He hath honour'd me of late; and I have bought Golden opinions from all sorts of people, Which would be worn now in their newest gloss, Not cast aside so soon. ❸

❶ Shakespeare uses this soliloquy to suggest that Macbeth still has some morality. The horse-jumping metaphor for ambition shows that he is aware that it will cause problems. He later ignores his own warning – a tragic convention.

❷ Shakespeare uses this dialogue to show Lady Macbeth's ability to control her husband and how her influence is part of his tragedy.

❸ Shakespeare uses visual metaphors here to show how Macbeth is fully aware of the situation, but soon after is persuaded by his wife. This indicates that his desire for power quickly outweighs his judgement shown here.

Knowledge

Knowledge — CHARACTERS

7 Macbeth

This takes place in Act 2 Scene 2, after Macbeth has murdered Duncan.

Lady Macbeth	Consider it not so deeply.
Macbeth	But wherefore could not I pronounce 'Amen'? I had most need of blessing, and 'Amen' Stuck in my throat. ❶
Lady Macbeth 5	These deeds must not be thought After these ways; so, it will make us mad. ❷
Macbeth	Methought I heard a voice cry, 'Sleep no more: Macbeth does murder sleep,' the innocent sleep, ❸

❶ Shakespeare focuses on Macbeth's despair, suggesting that evil actions result in a tragic isolation from God.

❷ Shakespeare contrasts his despair with his wife's dismissive attitude. These roles are reversed by the conclusion of the story.

❸ In this early phase of the play, Shakespeare shows that Macbeth feels immediate guilt and knows the evil of his actions as implied by the figurative use of 'innocent sleep'.

This takes place in Act 5 Scene 5, after Lady Macbeth has died.

Macbeth	She should have died hereafter; ❶ There would have been a time for such a word. Tomorrow, and tomorrow, and tomorrow Creeps in this petty pace from day to day
5	To the last syllable of recorded time; And all our yesterdays have lighted fools The way to dusty death. Out, out, brief candle, ❷ Life's but a walking shadow, a poor player That struts and frets his hour upon the stage
10	And then is heard no more. It is a tale Told by an idiot, full of sound and fury Signifying nothing. ❸

❶ Shakespeare uses this soliloquy to draw attention to Macbeth's tragic despair using figurative language to show how he feels life is joyless.

❷ These images also show Macbeth's feeling that life is just a preparation for death and that life is brief.

❸ Shakespeare piles up more images to show Macbeth's nihilism – all showing the end of his tragic journey, where he is forced to confront what he has become.

REMEMBER
The printed extract in the exam paper will tell you where in the play the extract has been taken from. It will also briefly tell you what has happened before the extract. Use this information to help you begin thinking about the point in the character's journey that you are focusing on.

REVISION TIP
Exam questions never ask you just to write about a character. They link a character to a key idea and either ask how it is presented or ask you to make a **judgement** upon it. When revising, always think about how characters' actions can be linked to ideas.

Key terms — Make sure you can write a definition for this key term: *judgement*

Writing about Macbeth

Sample answer 1: not a strong answer

Here is an extract from a student response to this question, with the examiner's annotations and final comments. It receives less than half marks.

> How far does Shakespeare present Macbeth as a character you can feel pity for?
>
> [30 marks]
> AO4 [4 marks]

❶ A vague opening, which isn't firmly focused on 'pity'

❸ There's a very loose sense that the writer's choices are being looked at, but the point made is a simple one.

> Readers can feel lots of things towards Macbeth. ❶ In the play he does lots of things that might make you pity him and lots of things that make you think he is just evil. ❷ In the printed scene, he says 'out, brief candle', which means that he wants things to be over quickly. ❸ It seems that he is not very happy by the end of the play and this means you can pity him. ❹

❷ This is a little better as the question is touched on, but it's still vague.

❹ A relevant but simple point about structure and ideas

Examiner's comments

The student does attempt to answer the question, but the ideas are simple and vague at times. There is a basic sense of the author's methods.

REMEMBER

- Do not spend time translating phrases. Assume that the examiner knows the plot of the play and what the words literally mean. Your job is to say something thoughtful about them.
- Your mark is largely determined by the quality of what you have to say – your thoughts and exploration of characters and ideas. Make sure you spend time exploring things in detail rather than skating over them.

# Knowledge

CHARACTERS

7 Macbeth

Sample answer 2: a strong answer

Here is an extract from a student response to this question, with the examiner's annotations and final comments. It receives high marks.

> How far does Shakespeare present Macbeth as a character you can feel pity for?
>
> [30 marks]
> AO4 [4 marks]

❶ The student begins by directly offering a view on the debate in the question.

> By the climax of the play, Macbeth has become a pitiable character. ❶ Shakespeare uses this soliloquy to show Macbeth's tragic realisation of the man he has become, where his wife's death prompts him to think about the worthlessness of life. ❷ Shakespeare uses a range of images to suggest that life means nothing – to Macbeth, it is simply a 'tale Told by an idiot'. This nihilistic view emphasises a key part of the tragic experience where the protagonist realises how his terrible errors have shaped him, and he is forced to come to terms with them. ❸ Macbeth does become worthy of pity by the end as his errors can only be undone by his death. The events in this part of the play reinforce the key moral message of the story – that those who transgress the rules will always pay the consequences. ❹

❷ A good sense of how methods are used to make a point about ideas

❸ The student makes a thoughtful point about tragedy, with a sense of how methods are used to do so.

❹ The student reinforces their view of the debate and links it to a big idea in the text.

Examiner's comments

This is a fluent, well-phrased response. The student directly addresses the question, makes points about the big ideas in the text, and has a good sense of how methods are used to show those ideas.

REMEMBER

- Know the key events that the character is part of.
- Understand how those events link to the big ideas of the text.
- Understand how methods are used to reveal character and ideas.

Retrieval

Answer the questions below. Cover the answers column with a piece of paper and write down as many answers as you can. Check and repeat.

Questions | Answers

1. Macbeth is presented as a brave and loyal character at the start of the play. True or false? — True

2. Briefly summarise the main points of Macbeth's journey. — A 'good' character who is tempted by ambition and betrays those who deserve his love, suffers as a consequence, and meets a deserved bloody end

3. What does Macbeth say is his only motivation to kill Duncan? — 'only Vaulting ambition which o'erleaps itself'

4. Give three key ideas emerging from Macbeth's journey. — Three from: Rampant ambition leads to terrible situations / Power corrupts people / People listen to what they want to hear / Terrible acts cause a loss of morality and feelings / A lust for power destroys relationships / Transgressors cannot escape punishment

5. In Act 1 Scene 7, Macbeth decides against killing Duncan. Why does he change his mind? — Lady Macbeth persuades him

6. Describe the contrasting attitudes of the Macbeths in Act 2 Scene 2 after the murder. — Macbeth despairs, and Lady Macbeth is dismissive

7. How does Macbeth react to his wife's suicide? — Without emotion

8. Exam questions never ask you just to write about a character. True or false? — True

9. Complete the quotation using two words. '"Macbeth does murder sleep", the _____,' — '"Macbeth does murder sleep", the innocent sleep,'

10. Complete the quotation using three words. 'Tomorrow, and tomorrow, and _____ Creeps in this _____.' — 'Tomorrow, and tomorrow, and tomorrow Creeps in this petty pace.'

Previous questions

Now go back and use these questions to check your knowledge of previous topics.

Questions | Answers

1. What does Banquo's ghost symbolise? — Macbeth's guilt

2. Give a basic definition of dramatic structure. — The order of events in the play

3. Give a moral message that emerges from Macbeth's death at the end of the play. — Those who go against the natural order won't get away with it

> Now turn to pages 98–100 and complete Practice questions 1–3.

Knowledge

CHARACTERS

8 Lady Macbeth

Key ideas of Lady Macbeth's journey

- Rampant ambition leads people to make terrible choices.
- Evil actions are often driven by a desire for power.
- Some characters can have a terrible influence on others.
- Evil acts can destroy relationships.
- Transgressors cannot escape punishment.

REMEMBER

Although Macbeth is the main tragic figure, Lady Macbeth also has her own tragic journey. Look back at the aspects of tragedy on page 2, and consider how they also fit Lady Macbeth's experiences.

REVISION TIP

Think about what Shakespeare shows you about characters' public behaviour and their private thoughts. Look at how dramatic irony and soliloquy are used to enhance your understanding of the personal tragedies that are unfolding.

Key events of Lady Macbeth's journey

① **Lady Macbeth plans to persuade her husband to kill Duncan.**
'Hie thee hither,
That I may pour my spirits in thine ear'

→ Shakespeare uses a soliloquy here to establish her as ambitious and conniving.

② **She requests help from dark forces to make her cruel.**
'take my milk for gall, you murd'ring ministers,'

→ This suggests that, like her husband, she makes a tragic error by deciding to commit a crime for power.

③ **She greets Duncan warmly while secretly plotting his murder.**
'All our service, In every point twice done and then done double,'

→ Dramatic irony here helps the audience to see her deceiving, cruel nature.

④ **She pressurises Macbeth to kill Duncan.**
'live a coward in thine own esteem'

→ In the early phase of the play, Shakespeare presents her as dominant.

⑤ **She frames Duncan's chamberlains for his murder.**
'If he do bleed,
I'll gild the faces of the grooms'

→ This is another indication of her cruel and decisive nature at this point in the story.

⑥ **She secretly expresses her growing unhappiness.**
'Nought's had, all's spent
Where our desire is got without content.'

→ Shakespeare uses this brief soliloquy to show a turning point in her story where she is now secretly unhappy.

8 Lady Macbeth

8

7 A distance grows between the Macbeths.

'How now, my lord, why do you keep alone,'

This is a turning point in the Macbeths' relationship, where he has started to not involve her in his plans.

8 She tries to excuse Macbeth's odd behaviour at the banquet.

'Pray you, keep seat.
The fit is momentary;'

Dramatic irony helps the audience see how she presents a composed manner in public while privately struggling.

9 She starts sleepwalking and hinting at the Macbeths' crimes.

'The Thane of Fife had a wife. Where is she now? What, will these hands ne'er be clean?'

Shakespeare uses her childlike rhymed speech and disconnected ideas to reveal her mental breakdown.

10 She kills herself.

'by self and violent hands
Took off her own life' (said by Malcolm)

Shakespeare uses Malcolm's final speech to reveal the truth of her death.

Key passages for Lady Macbeth

This takes place in Act 1 Scene 5, in which Lady Macbeth is persuading her husband to kill Duncan.

Lady Macbeth
O never
Shall sun that morrow see.
Your face, my thane, is as a book where men
May read strange matters. To beguile the time,
5   Look like the time; bear welcome in your eye,
Your hand, your tongue; look like th'innocent flower,
But be the serpent under't. ❶ He that's coming
Must be provided for, and you shall put ❷
This night's great business into my dispatch,
10 Which shall to all our nights and days to come
Give solely sovereign sway and masterdom.

Macbeth   We will speak further—

Lady Macbeth   Only look up ❷ clear;
To alter favour ever is to fear.
15 Leave ❷ all the rest to me. ❸

❶ Shakespeare uses the flower/serpent image to reveal her duplicity, and how she guides her husband to also be conniving.

❷ The use of **imperatives** suggests her dominance and confidence at this point in the play which contrasts with her later mental collapse.

❸ Shakespeare has given Lady Macbeth the bulk of the dialogue in this passage, suggesting her dominance.

Knowledge   37

Knowledge — CHARACTERS

8 Lady Macbeth

This dialogue is spoken to Macbeth in Act 1 Scene 7, when he refuses to kill Duncan.

Lady Macbeth   I have given suck, and know ❶
How tender 'tis to love the babe that milks me: ❷
I would, while it was smiling in my face,
Have pluck'd my nipple from his boneless gums
5 And dash'd the brains out, had I so sworn
As you have done to this.

❶ This brutal dialogue uses violent images as a way for Lady Macbeth to express her dismay at her husband. It further establishes her as a cruel and manipulative character.

❷ Shakespeare uses this image to echo ideas about innocence, which contrast with what follows after it.

This takes place in Act 3 Scene 2, before Banquo's murder.

Lady Macbeth   Nought's had, all's spent
Where our desire is got without content.
'Tis safer to be that which we destroy
Than by destruction dwell in doubtful joy. ❶
5 *Enter* Macbeth.

Lady Macbeth   How now, my lord, why do you keep alone,
Of sorriest fancies your companions making,
Using those thoughts which should indeed have died
With them they think on? Things without all remedy
10 Should be without regard; what's done, is done. ❷

❶ Shakespeare uses this brief soliloquy to reveal the misery Lady Macbeth feels – the first hint of her growing tragedy.

❷ Shakespeare uses Macbeth's entrance to suggest that Lady Macbeth acts differently when her husband arrives, pretending to be strong. This dramatic irony helps the audience to understand that she is crumbling internally.

> **REMEMBER**
> The actions and attitudes of characters are at the centre of any story. As you have seen on pages 24–27 what Shakespeare has the characters doing and saying is how the big ideas of the text emerge.

Key terms — Make sure you can write a definition for this key term: *imperative*

8 Lady Macbeth

8

Writing about Lady Macbeth

Sample answer 1: not a strong answer

Here is an extract from a student response to this question, with the examiner's annotations and final comments. It receives less than half marks.

> How far does Shakespeare present Lady Macbeth as a character you can feel pity for?
>
> **[30 marks]**
> **AO4 [4 marks]**

❶ Although there is some relevance here, the student is focusing on 'evil' rather than 'pity'.

❸ This isn't quite right – she says this about her husband.

> Lady Macbeth is an evil character who does many terrible things in the play. ❶ In the extract, she tells us that she is 'without content', which means she isn't satisfied. ❷ She also says that she feels 'alone'. ❸ Shakespeare has used words to show these things, and in some ways, it could make you pity her. ❹

❷ A relevant reference, but the student is just defining what it means rather than commenting on it.

❹ A basic awareness of method and some attempt to answer the question here.

Examiner's comments

This is a simple response that isn't always focused on the question. The student makes simple, general comments and comments vaguely on method.

REVISION TIP

The manner in which characters act and react towards each other gives a good guide to their feelings and attitudes. Look for parts of the play where these attitudes change or develop.

REMEMBER

'Sticking to the question' is essential. This means making sure that your answer is always relevant to the question. For instance, if the focus of the question is Lady Macbeth, don't spend time writing about her husband. When you write answers as part of your revision, read them and check that every paragraph is relevant to the question.

Knowledge

Knowledge — CHARACTERS

8 Lady Macbeth

Sample answer 2: a strong answer

Here is an extract from a student response to this question, with the examiner's annotations and final comments. It receives high marks.

> How far does Shakespeare present Lady Macbeth as a character you can feel pity for?
>
> [30 marks]
> AO4 [4 marks]

❶ An immediate response is given to the question.

❷ A specific and well-chosen reference is used to make a relevant point.

❸ This shows a sharp sense of how structural choices help meaning.

❹ A clear judgement on the debate is given.

> To an extent, Lady Macbeth arouses pity in the audience. ❶ As the play progresses, Shakespeare reveals that she is undergoing her own private tragedy, where she feels that it might be better to be 'that which we destroy' than suffer the misery they are experiencing. ❷ Shakespeare structures this scene so we are given a glimpse of her inner torment before he brings Macbeth into the action, where she reverts to her public display of strength. ❸ It's at this point in the play that the audience realises her bravado is an act and that, alongside her disintegrating marriage, she is starting to collapse. This does create some pity for her despite her otherwise evil actions. ❹

Examiner's comments

The student has directly addressed the question and focused on a specific piece of dialogue. There is good awareness of how structural choices reveal the character's feelings and the audience's response to them.

REMEMBER

In your exam you should:
- begin responses by offering an immediate response to the debate rather than writing general introductions. You can learn more about this on pages 86–97.
- directly address the question. Begin paragraphs by making a clear point that is relevant to the question, then develop your point using examples. It can help to restate your point at the end of the paragraph. You can see this in Sample answer 2.

40   8 Lady Macbeth

Retrieval

8

Answer the questions below. Cover the answers column with a piece of paper and write down as many answers as you can. Check and repeat.

Questions | Answers

#	Question	Answer
1	Lady Macbeth is unsure whether her husband should kill Duncan. True or false?	False
2	Explain how Lady Macbeth behaves publicly towards Duncan.	She greets Duncan warmly
3	Who does Lady Macbeth frame for Duncan's murder?	Duncan's chamberlains
4	Describe what happens to the Macbeths' relationship as the play progresses.	A distance grows between them
5	What happens to Lady Macbeth at the end of the play?	She kills herself
6	Give three key ideas emerging from Lady Macbeth's journey.	Three from: Rampant ambition leads people to make terrible choices / Evil actions are often driven by a desire for power / Some characters can have a terrible influence on others / Evil acts can destroy relationships / Transgressors cannot escape punishment
7	Explain how Lady Macbeth manipulates her husband to kill Duncan.	She accuses him of being a coward and emotionally blackmails him
8	Describe the contrast between Lady Macbeth's private thoughts and her public behaviour.	In private, she feels that their efforts have been wasted; in public, she affects a positive and encouraging manner
9	Complete the quotation. 'look like the _____, but the _____ under't.'	'look like the <u>flower</u>, but be the <u>serpent</u> under't.'
10	Complete the quotation using three words. 'Have pluck'd my nipple from his _____ And _____ the brains out,'	'Have pluck'd my nipple from his <u>boneless gums</u> And <u>dash'd</u> the brains out,'

Previous questions

Now go back and use these questions to check your knowledge of previous topics.

Questions | Answers

#	Question	Answer
1	Macbeth is presented as a brave and loyal character at the start of the play. True or false?	True
2	What does Macbeth say is his only motivation to kill Duncan?	'only Vaulting ambition which o'erleaps itself'

> ✎ Now turn to pages 101–104 and complete Practice questions 4–7.

Retrieval

Knowledge — CHARACTERS

9 The witches

Key ideas of the witches' journey

- Evil influences can destroy good people through encouraging ambition.
- A powerful man can be controlled by powerless social outcasts.
- Words and suggestion can bring about the downfall of very powerful figures.
- The supernatural is a mysterious and powerful force.

> **REVISION TIP**
>
> It's unlikely that an exam question will be about the witches in isolation, but you need to know their relationship with Macbeth and how their actions link to the ideas of the text. The same is true for Macduff, Banquo, Duncan, and Malcolm.

Key events of the witches' journey

1 The three witches meet in a storm and arrange to meet Macbeth.
'Fair is foul, and foul is fair,'
— Shakespeare's use of a stormy isolated **setting** associates the witches with chaos.

2 The first witch describes torturing a sailor.
'He shall live a man forbid.'
— Shakespeare uses the **backstory** of the tortured sailor to show the witches' malevolence and suggest how they might affect Macbeth.

3 They meet Macbeth and seem to predict his future and that of Banquo's sons.
'that shalt be king hereafter.'
— This is a key turning point in the story, where Macbeth's ambitions are awakened and a split starts to form between Banquo and Macbeth.

4 The witches' predictions lead Macbeth and his wife to commit murder.
'As the weïrd women promis'd', (said by Banquo)
— Shakespeare shows how the witches' influence plays out, suggesting that words have power.

5 The first witch meets Hecate (queen of witches), who plots to confuse Macbeth further.
'Shall draw him on to his confusion.' (said by Hecate)
— Shakespeare uses this scene to remind the audience that Macbeth is being deliberately played with.

6 Using apparitions, the witches offer further predictions to Macbeth about the future.

'Enter a show of eight kings' (stage direction)

Shakespeare associates the witches with a lot of dramatic spectacle – apparitions, storms, vanishings – to emphasise their otherworldly qualities.

7 Macbeth realises too late that he has been tricked by the witches.

'these juggling fiends' (said by Macbeth)

This late realisation in the resolution of the play is a key part of Macbeth's tragedy.

Key passages for the witches

This takes place in Act 1 Scene 1, in which the witches arrange to meet Macbeth.

First Witch		When shall we three meet again?
		In thunder, lightning, or in rain? ❶
Second Witch		When the hurly-burly's done,
		When the battle's lost, and won.
Third Witch	5	That will be ere the set of sun.
First Witch		Where the place?
Second Witch		Upon the heath.
Third Witch		There to meet with Macbeth.
First Witch		I come, Graymalkin.
Second Witch	10	Paddock calls. ❷
Third Witch		Anon.
All		Fair is foul, and foul is fair,
		Hover through the fog and filthy air. ❸

❶ Shakespeare places the witches in isolated, stormy settings, in contrast to the other scenes which occur in powerful places such as castles.

❷ The witches' ability to speak to animals and know when the battle will end signifies their strange qualities.

❸ These final lines suggest things that appear good are in fact evil, suggesting a link to the way Macbeth interprets the witches' predictions.

Knowledge

Knowledge

CHARACTERS

9 The witches

This dialogue takes place in Act 1 Scene 3, when Macbeth and Banquo meet the witches for the first time.

Macbeth	So foul and fair a day I have not seen. ❶
Banquo	How far is't call'd to Forres? What are these, So wither'd and so wild in their attire, That look not like the inhabitants o'th'earth, ❷
	5 And yet are on't?—Live you, or are you aught That man may question? You seem to understand me, By each at once her choppy finger laying Upon her skinny lips; you should be women, And yet your beards forbid me to interpret
	10 That you are so.
Macbeth	Speak, if you can: what are you?
First Witch	All hail Macbeth, hail to thee, Thane of Glamis.
Second Witch	All hail Macbeth, hail to thee, Thane of Cawdor. ❸
Third Witch	All hail Macbeth, that shalt be king hereafter.

❶ These words echo the witches' final line in Act 1 Scene 1 and may suggest the witches already have some sort of influence over Macbeth.

❷ Shakespeare has Banquo describe the witches' unusual appearance to suggest that they are abnormal.

❸ The audience already knows that Macbeth will be made Thane of Cawdor, but Macbeth doesn't at this point.

> **REVISION TIP**
>
> With more minor characters, it is important to look closely at their relationship with main characters – how their words and actions have influence, and how their values and conduct contrast with those of main characters.

Key terms — Make sure you can write a definition for these key terms: backstory, setting

Retrieval

9

Answer the questions below. Cover the answers column with a piece of paper and write down as many answers as you can. Check and repeat.

Questions | Answers

#	Question	Answer
1	Describe the weather in the opening scene and what it suggests about the witches.	A storm, which associates them with chaos
2	How do the witches' words influence Macbeth?	They predict his future, leading the Macbeths to plan murder
3	Who is Hecate?	Queen of witches
4	Complete the quotation using two words. (stage direction) 'Enter a show of _____'	'Enter a show of eight kings'
5	Macbeth never realises that he has been tricked by the witches. True or false?	False
6	It's unlikely that an exam question will ask you solely about the witches. True or false?	True
7	Complete the quotation using five words. 'When shall we three meet again? In _____?'	'When shall we three meet again? In thunder, lightning, or in rain?'
8	Explain what 'foul is fair' means.	Things that appear good are in fact evil
9	How does Banquo describe the witches' attire (clothing)?	'So wither'd and so wild'
10	The audience knows that Macbeth will be made Thane of Cawdor before he does. True or false?	True

Previous questions

Now go back and use these questions to check your knowledge of previous topics.

Questions | Answers

#	Question	Answer
1	Complete the quotation using four words. 'It is a tale Told by an _____, full of _____, Signifying nothing.'	'It is a tale Told by an idiot, full of sound and fury Signifying nothing.'
2	Lady Macbeth is unsure whether her husband should kill Duncan. True or false?	False
3	Who does Lady Macbeth frame for Duncan's murder?	Duncan's chamberlains
4	Complete the quotation using three words. 'Have pluck'd my nipple from his _____ And _____ the brains out,'	'Have pluck'd my nipple from his boneless gums And dash'd the brains out,'

 Knowledge — CHARACTERS

10 Macduff

Key ideas of Macduff's journey

- Loyalty and commitment cause people to act selflessly.
- Principles rather than ambition can govern human behaviour.
- Legitimate rulers are eventually restored to power.

> **REVISION TIP**
> Drama texts rely partly on performance for interpretation. Watch different film versions of the same scene and the different effects created. For example, some of Macduff's early lines spoken to Macbeth might be spoken in either a respectful or a suspicious manner.

Key events of Macduff's journey

1. Macduff arrives and discovers Duncan's body.
'Most sacrilegious murder hath broke ope
The Lord's anointed temple'

Shakespeare contrasts Macduff's shock and love for Duncan with Macbeth's selfish brutality.

2. Macduff avoids going to see Macbeth being crowned.
'our old robes sit easier than our new'

Shakespeare uses clothing imagery to suggest Macduff thinks Macbeth's reign will be less comfortable than Duncan's.

3. Macbeth notes that Macduff didn't attend the banquet.
'Macduff denies his person
At our great bidding?' (said by Macbeth)

Here, Shakespeare signals the growing distrust between the two men.

4. The witches' apparitions warn Macbeth to be wary of Macduff, after which he orders the murder of Macduff's family.
'beware Macduff,
Beware the Thane of Fife.'

Shakespeare uses this scene to reinforce Macbeth's reliance on the witches and the tragic consequences for Macduff.

5. Macduff describes the terrible reign of Macbeth to Malcolm.
'Not in the legions
Of horrid hell can come a devil more damn'd In evils'

Shakespeare uses this long scene to reinforce Macduff's unselfish loyalty to Scotland.

6. Macduff promises to seek revenge on Macbeth for his family's murder.
'Within my sword's length set him.'

Here, Shakespeare sets up Macduff as a revenging figure.

10

7 Macduff fights Macbeth, during which Macduff reveals he was born by caesarean section.

'Macduff was from his mother's womb Untimely ripp'd.'

— This revelation echoes the witches' words and seals Macbeth's fate.

8 Macduff decapitates Macbeth and proclaims Malcolm the rightful king.

'Behold where stands Th'usurper's cursed head.'

— This event is a key moment in the resolution of the tragedy.

> **REMEMBER**
> Remember that characters can also be thought about in terms of their function. For example, Macduff can be viewed as being a revenger figure in the play's structure.

Key passages for Macduff

This takes place in Act 2 Scene 3 when Macduff discovers Duncan's body.

Macduff   Approach the chamber and destroy your sight
With a new Gorgon. ❶ Do not bid me speak:
See and then speak yourselves.
[*Exeunt* Macbeth *and* Lennox.]
5   Awake, awake!
Ring the alarum bell! Murder and treason!
Banquo and Donaldbain! Malcolm, awake,
Shake off this downy sleep, death's counterfeit,
And look on death itself. Up, up, and see
10   The great doom's image. Malcolm, Banquo,
As from your graves rise up and walk like sprites
To countenance this horror. ❷

Bell rings. Enter Lady Macbeth.

Lady Macbeth   What's the business
15   That such a hideous trumpet calls to parley
The sleepers of the house? Speak, speak.

Macduff   O gentle lady,
Tis not for you to hear what I can speak. ❸

❶ Shakespeare uses mythical imagery here to present the depth of Macduff's horror.

❷ The use of **exclamations** and imperatives in Macduff's speech shows the energy and drama of his feelings and the magnitude of the murder.

❸ Dramatic irony allows the audience to see Lady Macbeth's play-acting in contrast to Macduff's genuine horror.

Knowledge 47

Knowledge — CHARACTERS

10 Macduff

This dialogue is spoke in Act 4 Scene 3 after Macduff learns of his family's murder.

Macduff	Did heaven look on,
	And would not take their part? Sinful Macduff,
	They were all struck for thee. Naught that I am,
	Not for their own demerits but for mine,
5	Fell slaughter on their souls. Heaven rest them now. ❶
Malcolm	Be this the whetstone of your sword, let grief
	Convert to anger. Blunt not the heart, enrage it. ❷
Macduff	O, I could play the woman with mine eyes
	And braggart with my tongue. But gentle heavens,
10	Cut short all intermission. Front to front
	Bring thou this fiend of Scotland and myself;
	Within my sword's length set him. If he scape,
	Heaven forgive him too. ❸

❶ Shakespeare initiates a contrast between Macduff's emotional response to his family's murder and Macbeth's indifferent response to his wife's death in the next act.

❷ Macduff is set up as a revenging figure who is placed firmly in opposition to Macbeth.

❸ The strength and intent of these words reinforce Macduff's emotional character.

REVISION TIP

When exploring the function of characters, consider which ones cause disorder and which ones help to re-establish order.

REMEMBER

Tragedy is about the downfall of a powerful character. During this downfall, there are key moments where the character's death becomes inevitable. Macduff's desire for revenge is one such moment.

Key terms — Make sure you can write a definition for this key term: exclamation

Retrieval

10

Answer the questions below. Cover the answers column with a piece of paper and write down as many answers as you can. Check and repeat.

Questions | Answers

1. Macduff discovers Duncan's body. True or false? | True
2. Give two public occasions involving Macbeth that Macduff doesn't attend. | The crowning and the banquet
3. Who tells Macbeth to 'beware Macduff'? | The witches' apparitions
4. Complete the quotation using three words. 'Not in the legions Of _____ can come a devil more _____ In evils' | 'Not in the legions Of horrid hell can come a devil more damn'd In evils'
5. What prompts Macduff's revenge? | His family's murder
6. Complete the quotation. 'Bring thou this fiend of Scotland and myself; Within my _____ length set him.' | 'Bring thou this fiend of Scotland and myself; Within my sword's length set him.'
7. What is the significance of Macduff's caesarean birth? | It echoes the witches' words and seals Macbeth's fate
8. Macduff cuts off Macbeth's head. True or false? | True
9. Give three ideas emerging from Macduff's journey. | Loyalty and commitment cause people to act selflessly; principles rather than ambition can govern human behaviour; legitimate rulers are eventually restored to power
10. How does Macduff's response to Duncan's death contrast with Lady Macbeth's response? | Dramatic irony allows the audience to see Lady Macbeth's play-acting in contrast to Macduff's horror

Previous questions

Now go back and use these questions to check your knowledge of previous topics.

Questions | Answers

1. Describe what happens to the Macbeths' relationship as the play progresses. | A distance grows between them
2. Who is Hecate? | Queen of witches
3. Macbeth never realises that he has been tricked by the witches. True or false? | False
4. Complete the quotation using two words. (stage direction) 'Enter a show of _____' | 'Enter a show of eight kings'

Retrieval 49

Knowledge

CHARACTERS

11 Banquo

Key ideas of Banquo's journey

- Power and ambition can destroy trust.
- Characters respond to temptation in contrasting ways.
- Morally wrong acts return to haunt the transgressor.

Key events of Banquo's journey

1 Banquo acts bravely alongside Macbeth to defend Duncan in the battle.

'So they doubly redoubled strokes upon the foe.' (said by the Captain)

— Shakespeare establishes Banquo's loyalty and closeness to Macbeth in the opening act.

2 The witches predict his sons will rule Scotland.

'Thou shalt get kings, though thou be none.' (said by Third Witch)

— Shakespeare has Macbeth hear these predictions, which become a source of torment for him as the play progresses.

3 He warns Macbeth not to trust the witches.

'to win us to our harm,
The instruments of darkness tell us truths;'

— Shakespeare shows the contrast between the men's reactions, suggesting that Banquo is more cautious.

4 He agrees to discuss the witches' predictions with Macbeth, as long as it doesn't cause him loss of honour.

'…keep
My bosom franchis'd and allegiance clear,'

— Here Shakespeare emphasises Banquo's noble and moral qualities.

5 He suspects Macbeth of murdering Duncan.

'I fear
Thou play'd most foully for't;'

— This soliloquy shows the growing divide between the characters.

6 Macbeth orders the death of Banquo and Fleance, but Fleance escapes.

'thy soul's flight, If it find heaven, must find it out tonight.' (said by Macbeth)

— These orders show how Macbeth has lost his conscience – he has no doubts about what he is doing now.

7 Banquo's bloodied ghost appears to Macbeth at the banquet.

'never shake
Thy gory locks at me!' (said by Macbeth)

— Shakespeare uses Banquo's ghost as a symbol of Macbeth's guilt, suggesting it is impossible for him to ignore what he has done.

8 Banquo's ghost appears when Macbeth visits the witches for the second time.

'For the blood-bolter'd Banquo smiles upon me' (said by Macbeth)

— Shakespeare presents Banquo as laughing at Macbeth here, another symbol of Macbeth's inability to put an end to his fears for the future.

Key passages for Banquo

This takes place in Act 1 Scene 3, after the witches have given their predictions and Macbeth has been made Thane of Cawdor.

Macbeth	[*Aside.*] Glamis, and Thane of Cawdor: The greatest is behind. ❶ —Thanks for your pains.— [*To* Banquo.] Do you not hope your children shall be kings, When those that gave the Thane of Cawdor to me
5	Promis'd no less to them? ❷
Banquo	That trusted home, Might yet enkindle you unto the crown, Besides the Thane of Cawdor. But 'tis strange, And oftentimes, to win us to our harm,
10	The instruments of darkness tell us truths; Win us with honest trifles, to betray's In deepest consequence. ❸

❶ This aside sets up a contrast between Macbeth's private thoughts and Banquo's subsequent rejection of the witches' words.

❷ Now the audience knows what Macbeth is really thinking, this line might be read as a test of Banquo's loyalty and possible threat to Macbeth's future.

❸ Shakespeare draws a contrast between Macbeth's desire for power and Banquo's more measured response – which later proves true.

This is spoken at the start of Act 3 Scene 1, before Macbeth enters.

Banquo	Thou hast it now, King, Cawdor, Glamis, all, As the weïrd women promis'd, and, I fear Thou played'st most foully for't; ❶ yet it was said It should not stand in thy posterity,
5	But that myself should be the root and father Of many kings. If there come truth from them— As upon thee, Macbeth, their speeches shine— Why by the verities on thee made good, May they not be my oracles as well
10	And set me up in hope? ❷ But hush, no more. ❸

❶ This soliloquy reveals Banquo's private suspicions and signifies his growing distrust.

❷ This private admission suggests that Banquo hopes the witches' words might be true for his family, but crucially he doesn't act upon them – a contrast to Macbeth.

❸ Banquo dismisses his brief ambitious thoughts – this might suggest he has some moral scruples.

> **REMEMBER**
>
> Many lines and actions can be read in different ways. Thinking about the ways you can interpret things opens up a range of meanings – but always make sure they make logical sense in light of what happens elsewhere in the play.

> **REVISION TIP**
>
> When exploring the relationships between characters, explore the moments where their attitudes towards each other change or develop. Consider the turning points in their relationship.

Retrieval

Answer the questions below. Cover the answers column with a piece of paper and write down as many answers as you can. Check and repeat.

Questions / Answers

#	Questions	Answers
1	The witches predict Banquo will become king. True or false?	False
2	Describe Banquo's initial response to the witches' words.	He warns Macbeth not to trust the witches
3	Complete the quotation. 'And oftentimes, to win us to our _____, The instruments of darkness tell us _____;'	'And oftentimes, to win us to our harm, The instruments of darkness tell us truths;'
4	How does Banquo respond when Macbeth asks to discuss the witches' words?	He agrees, as long as it doesn't cause him loss of honour
5	Complete the quotation using two words. 'I fear Thou played'st _____ for't;'	'I fear Thou played'st most foully for't;'
6	Give two occasions where Banquo's ghost appears.	At the banquet and when Macbeth visits the witches again
7	What might Banquo's ghost symbolise?	Macbeth's guilt
8	Give three key ideas emerging from Banquo's journey.	How power and ambition can destroy trust; the contrasting way characters respond to temptation; how morally wrong acts return to haunt the transgressor
9	Explain how Banquo's trust in Macbeth changes.	He grows to suspect Macbeth of being influenced by the witches and playing 'most foully' to become king
10	Banquo secretly hopes his children will become kings. True or false?	True

Previous questions

Now go back and use these questions to check your knowledge of previous topics.

#	Questions	Answers
1	What happens to Lady Macbeth at the end?	She kills herself
2	Describe the weather in the opening scene and what it suggests about the witches.	A storm, which associates them with chaos
3	Macduff discovers Duncan's body. True or false?	True
4	Who tells Macbeth to 'beware Macduff'?	The witches' apparitions
5	Complete the quotation using three words. 'Not in the legions Of _____ can come a devil more _____ In evils'	'Not in the legions Of horrid hell can come a devil more damn'd In evils'

11 Banquo

Knowledge — CHARACTERS — 12

12 Duncan and Malcolm

Key ideas of Duncan and Malcolm's journeys

- Responsible use of power creates loyalty and a settled world.
- Good men can become victims of power-hungry characters.
- Order and stability return in the end and the guilty are punished.

Key events of Duncan and Malcolm's journey

1. Duncan rewards Macbeth for his loyalty and bravery.
'O valiant cousin, worthy gentleman.'
— This establishes Duncan as a character who uses his power to encourage loyalty.

2. Duncan says you can't judge loyalty from outward appearance.
'There's no art
To find the mind's construction in the face.'
— These lines establish a main idea of the play about trust and deception.

3. Macbeth accepts Duncan is a good king and he shouldn't kill him, and yet he still does.
'this Duncan
Hath borne his faculties so meek' (said by Macbeth)
— Shakespeare uses Macbeth's soliloquy to foreground the problems of ambition when it means sacrificing a good man for a lust for power.

4. Malcolm suspects that Macbeth's grief is an act and flees to England.
'an unfelt sorrow is an office
Which the false man does easy.'
— Malcolm's immediate response to his father's murder reveals his ability to perceive danger and falsehood.

5. Malcolm finally accepts Macduff's request to help him defeat Macbeth.
'What I am truly Is thine, and my poor country's, to command:'
— Shakespeare uses this long scene to reinforce Malcolm as a thoughtful and cautious character with a sense of moral purpose.

6. Malcolm resolves to attack Macbeth.
'...Macbeth
Is ripe for shaking, and the powers above
Put on their instruments.'
— Malcolm's desire to unseat Macbeth echoes Macbeth's usurpation of Duncan at the start of the play.

7. Macduff proclaims Malcolm King of Scotland.
'Hail, king, for so thou art.' (said by Macduff)
— Malcolm's ascendancy to the throne signifies a return to the rightful order.

8. Malcolm promotes all of the thanes.
'My thanes and kinsmen,
Henceforth be earls,'
— This suggests Malcolm will use his power to encourage loyalty, echoing his father's actions in Act 1.

Knowledge — CHARACTERS

12 Duncan and Malcolm

Key passages for Duncan and Malcolm

This takes place in Act 1 Scene 7, while Duncan and his followers are at dinner at Macbeth's castle.

Macbeth
He's here in double trust:
First, as I am his kinsman and his subject,
Strong both against the deed; then, as his host,
Who should against his murderer shut the door,
5 Not bear the knife myself. ❶ Besides, this Duncan
Hath borne his faculties so meek, hath been
So clear in his great office, that his virtues
Will plead like angels, trumpet-tongu'd against
The deep damnation of his taking-off.
10 And pity, like a naked new-born babe
Striding the blast, or heaven's cherubin hors'd
Upon the sightless couriers of the air, ❷
Shall blow the horrid deed in every eye,
That tears shall drown the wind. I have no spur
15 To prick the sides of my intent, but only
Vaulting ambition which o'erleaps itself
And falls on th'other — ❸

❶ Shakespeare uses this soliloquy to reinforce ideas about Duncan's status and why Macbeth should be loyal.

❷ Religious images are used here to align Duncan with God and suggest his nobility.

❸ Shakespeare uses this part to show how Macbeth's selfishness will outweigh any of Duncan's good qualities.

This dialogue is spoken in the final lines of Act 5 Scene 9, after Malcolm has been named king.

Malcolm
We shall not spend a large expense of time
Before we reckon with your several loves
And make us even with you. My thanes and kinsmen,
Henceforth be earls, the first that ever Scotland
5 In such an honour nam'd. ❶ What's more to do
Which would be planted newly with the time,—
As calling home our exil'd friends abroad
That fled the snares of watchful tyranny,
Producing forth the cruel ministers
10 Of this dead butcher and his fiend-like queen, ❷
Who, as 'tis thought, by self and violent hands
Took off her life,—this and what needful else
That calls upon us, by the grace of Grace
We will perform in measure, time, and place. ❸
15 So thanks to all at once and to each one,
Whom we invite to see us crown'd at Scone. ❹

❶ This final speech is used by Shakespeare to show that a new order is being established in the resolution of the play.

❷ Shakespeare gives Malcolm the final judgement on the Macbeths.

❸ Malcolm appears to have the same noble qualities as his father.

❹ These words present Malcolm as an inclusive and civil new king.

REVISION TIP
Look at how linked characters, such as those from the same family, are used to suggest contrasts or points of comparison that link to the big ideas.

REVISION TIP
Consider which characters have power by the end, and which have lost it. Look at suggestions of how they will use their power and what it suggests for the future.

Retrieval 12

Answer the questions below. Cover the answers column with a piece of paper and write down as many answers as you can. Check and repeat.

Questions | Answers

#	Questions	Answers
1	Why does Duncan reward Macbeth?	For his loyalty and bravery
2	Who says 'There's no art To find the mind's construction in the face', and what does it mean?	Duncan; you can't judge loyalty from outward appearance
3	What is Macbeth's impression of Duncan prior to killing him?	He is a good king
4	Complete the quotation. 'this Duncan Hath borne his faculties so _____,'	'this Duncan Hath borne his faculties so meek,'
5	Where does Malcolm flee to in the aftermath of his father's murder?	England
6	Who accepts Macduff's request to help him defeat Macbeth?	Malcolm
7	What does Malcolm offer the thanes at the end of the play?	He promotes them (to earls)
8	Complete the quotation. 'My thanes and kinsmen, Henceforth be _____,'	'My thanes and kinsmen, Henceforth be earls,'
9	Give three ideas that emerge from the journeys of Duncan and Malcolm.	Responsible use of power creates loyalty and a settled world; good men can become victims of power-hungry characters; order and stability return in the end and the guilty are punished
10	Malcolm appears to have the same noble qualities as his father. True or false?	True

Previous questions

Now go back and use these questions to check your knowledge of previous topics.

#	Questions	Answers
1	How do the witches' words influence Macbeth?	They predict his future, leading the Macbeths to plan murder
2	What prompts Macduff's revenge?	His family's murder
3	The witches predict Banquo will become king. True or false?	False
4	What might Banquo's ghost symbolise?	Macbeth's guilt

Knowledge — THEMES

13 Ambition

The ideas of a text – what the text is 'about' – are sometimes called 'themes'. When you study a text, the events and characters' actions combine to reveal ideas about things such as power, morality, evil, and deception.

Ambition

Ambition means the desire to achieve something. In real life, ambition is often a good thing. In *Macbeth*, selfish ambition is shown to be a bad thing that has consequences.

> **REVISION TIP**
> Make sure you are confident about plot and characters before you look closely at themes. Knowing the details of the play will make revising themes much easier.

Key events involving ambition

Macbeth

- The witches' words awaken Macbeth's desire to be king.

- Macbeth's ambition is initially thwarted when he finds out that Malcolm is the next intended king.

- Macbeth realises that his ambitions aren't morally good.

- Macbeth knows that he shouldn't pursue his ambitions, but makes the tragic error of doing so.

- When he becomes king, it brings Macbeth misery rather than joy.

- Macbeth comes to realise that his ambitions have led him to his tragic end.

- Macbeth's pursuit of his ambitions leads ultimately to his death.

> **REVISION TIP**
> Ideas and themes develop during the course of a story – new events and characters' decisions add further layers to a theme. Look for key moments in a story where something significant happens that adds to a theme.

Other characters

- Banquo has ambitions for his children, but maintains his integrity.
- Lady Macbeth has ambitions for her husband and acts immorally to achieve them.
- Lady Macbeth's pursuit of ambition also leads her to misery and death.
- Macduff has a selfless ambition to help Scotland get rid of Macbeth.
- Malcolm has ambitions to be a good king.

13

Five key lines about ambition

Lines	What they show about ambition
'why do I yield to that suggestion, Whose horrid image doth unfix my hair And make my seated heart knock at my ribs' (Act 1 Scene 3)	These references to his physical response to the thought of killing Duncan show that Macbeth realises his ambitions are wrong. He tragically ignores this warning from his own conscience and foolishly pursues his selfish desires.
[Aside] 'Stars, hide your fires, Let not light see my black and deep desires,' (Act 1 Scene 4)	These words are spoken after Macbeth hears that Malcolm is the next intended king. Shakespeare uses this aside and the dark imagery to show that Macbeth fully realises his ambitions are immoral and must not be spoken about publicly.
'Thou wouldst be great, Art not without ambition, but without The illness should attend it.' (Act 1 Scene 5)	Shakespeare uses Lady Macbeth's soliloquy to show her private worries that her husband lacks the cruelty to pursue his ambitions. This shows she is fully aware that dangerous ambitions are linked to ideas about selfishness and evil.
'I have no spur To prick the sides of my intent, but only Vaulting ambition which o'erleaps itself And falls on th'other—' (Act 1 Scene 7)	Shakespeare's use of this horse-jumping metaphor shows that Macbeth realises that he is motivated by ambition but that it is a big risk, which may end in disaster. He also ignores this warning from his conscience.
'Bring thou this fiend of Scotland and myself. Within my sword's length set him.' (Act 4 Scene 3)	Macduff's dramatic dialogue reveals an ambition for revenge, which many audiences would see as justified and morally right, given Macbeth's actions.

Five key points about ambition

1. Selfish ambition is a terrible thing that causes people to act immorally.
2. Selfish ambition can destroy people, relationships, and countries.
3. Ambition is a tragic flaw, which leads to suffering.
4. Characters who pursue selfish ambitions can't escape the consequence of death.
5. Selfless ambition to restore order is a positive thing.

REMEMBER
The most thoughtful responses always get to the heart of what is being shown about an idea. Use the 'five key points' list to remind you of the best points to include in an idea-based question.

Knowledge

Knowledge — THEMES

13 Ambition

Writing about ambition

Sample answer 1: not a strong answer

Here is an extract from a student response to this question, with the examiner's annotations and final comments. It receives less than half marks.

> How does Shakespeare present ideas about ambition?
>
> [30 marks]
> AO4 [4 marks]

> Ambition means wanting to achieve things and in the play there are lots of characters with ambitions, some bad, some good. ❶ Macbeth himself has an ambition to be king and he kills for it, which is a bad thing. His wife is also ambitious, and she persuades him to do it. Both of these people end up dead. ❷ There are other characters with good ambitions such as Macduff, who wants to kill Macbeth. He achieves this by the end, which audiences like. ❸

❶ A relevant but simple point

❷ Identifies relevant examples of ambition, but the comment is simple

❸ Another relevant but underdeveloped example

Examiner's comments

Relevant examples of ambition are given, but the accompanying comments are simple. There is very little sense of Shakespeare's methods.

REMEMBER

There is no need to define terms. For example, when answering this question, you don't need to define ambition. Assume that your examiner knows such concepts. Your job is to say thoughtful things about these concepts.

REVISION TIP

Your marks will mainly depend on how thoughtful your points are. When practising answering questions, always develop and explain your thoughts.

13

Sample answer 2: a strong answer

Here is an extract from a student response to this question, with the examiner's annotations and final comments. It receives high marks.

> How does Shakespeare present ideas about ambition?
>
> [30 marks]
> AO4 [4 marks]

❶ A good awareness of how method is used to show a key idea about ambition, with a specific and relevant reference

Shakespeare uses the character of Macbeth to show what happens when ambition runs wild. Early soliloquies reveal that Macbeth realises what he's doing is wrong and that his 'black and deep desires' must remain hidden, yet he still goes ahead and commits the tragic error that leads to his downfall. ❶ Shakespeare uses Macbeth's journey to show how, by the play's resolution, ambition has led Macbeth to a sense of futility and misery. ❷ Ultimately, the play's moral ideas are conservative: it encourages audiences to not give in to ill ambitions, else face the consequences. ❸

❷ A perceptive point about the wider effect of ambition

❸ Another perceptive point about the meaning of ambition in the play

Examiner's comments

Very insightful points are made about what the play reveals about ambition. A good grasp of various methods is shown, and the response is written in fluent English.

REMEMBER

- It's often better to write about structural methods as they usually lead more naturally to points about the ideas in a text. You can see this in Sample answer 2.
- A perceptive point is one that shows high-level thinking. This is why it is best to think and plan before you start writing – time spent gathering your thoughts before you begin a response is time well spent.

REVISION TIP

Thinking about big concepts such as morality can help you raise the quality of your thinking and writing. Focusing on what the end of a text has to say about human conduct is a good place to start. You can see an example of this in Sample answer 2.

Knowledge 59

Retrieval

Answer the questions below. Cover the answers column with a piece of paper and write down as many answers as you can. Check and repeat.

Questions	Answers
1. Whose words awaken Macbeth's ambitions?	The witches'
2. Macbeth is unaware that his ambitions are morally wrong. True or false?	False
3. Macbeth's ambitions cause unhappiness. True or false?	True
4. Describe Lady Macbeth's ambitions.	She desires the power that would result from her husband becoming king
5. Describe Macduff's ambitions.	A selfless ambition to help Scotland get rid of Macbeth
6. Complete the quotation. 'Stars, hide your _____, Let not light see my ____ and _____ desires'	'Stars, hide your fires, Let not light see my black and deep desires'
7. Complete the quotation. 'Art not without _____, but without The _____ should attend it.'	'Art not without ambition, but without The illness should attend it.'
8. What method is used in the phrase 'vaulting ambition'?	Metaphor
9. What does the line 'Vaulting ambition which o'erleaps itself' show about Macbeth's attitude towards ambition?	Macbeth realises that he is motivated by ambition but that it is a big risk, which may end in disaster
10. Give three key points about ambition shown in the play.	Three from: Selfish ambition is a terrible thing that causes people to act immorally / Selfish ambition can destroy people, relationships, and countries / Ambition is a tragic flaw, which leads to suffering / Characters who pursue selfish ambitions can't escape the consequence of death / Selfless ambition to restore order is a positive thing

Previous questions

Now go back and use these questions to check your knowledge of previous topics.

Questions	Answers
1. How does Macbeth react to his wife's suicide?	Without emotion
2. What might Banquo's ghost symbolise?	Macbeth's guilt

Now turn to page 105 and complete Practice question 8.

13 Ambition

 # Knowledge THEMES  14

14 Power

Power

'Power' means the ability to influence the behaviour of others. The play shows how power is gained, maintained, and lost. It explores ideas about how kings and other characters use their powers.

> **REVISION TIP**
> Be alert to how exam questions might use close synonyms for some of the ideas explored in this book. For example, a question about 'control' will have obvious links to ideas about 'power'.

> **REMEMBER**
> Many themes and ideas in the play overlap. For example, ambition has obvious links to power. Be comfortable with seeing ideas as interactive.

Key events involving power

- King Duncan uses his power thoughtfully and rewards loyalty.
- The witches appear socially powerless, but have power over Macbeth.
- Macbeth seeks power and achieves it by violent means.
- Lady Macbeth seeks power and requests the aid of dark forces to achieve it.
- Achieving power does not make the Macbeths happy.
- Macbeth abuses his power and maintains it through murder.
- Macbeth is a terrible king who loses the support of the thanes.
- Macduff and Malcolm use combined powers to attack Macbeth.
- Lady Macbeth dies, so the way she pursues power has caused her to suffer.
- Macbeth loses his power at the end of the play and dies.
- Malcolm, the rightful king, gains power at the end, and there is a return to order.
- Malcolm appears to have the makings of a good king who will use his power wisely.

Retrieval

Knowledge — THEMES

14 Power

Five key lines about power

Lines	What they show about power
'this Duncan Hath borne his faculties so meek, hath been So clear in his great office, that his virtues Will plead like angels,' (Act 1 Scene 7)	Shakespeare uses this soliloquy to **characterise** Duncan as a good, moral king, who uses power wisely. He has previously awarded Macbeth the title 'Thane of Cawdor' for loyalty and bravery. The **simile** 'like angels' suggests that God is on Duncan's side.
'Come, you spirits That tend on mortal thoughts, unsex me here And fill me from the crown to the toe top-full Of direst cruelty;' (Act 1 Scene 5)	This soliloquy establishes Lady Macbeth's need and wish for the powers of evil to help her in her pursuit of power. It implies that her feminine qualities are not helpful in achieving her desires.
'Better be with the dead Whom we, to gain our peace, have sent to peace, Than on the torture of the mind to lie In restless ecstasy.' (Act 3 Scene 2)	Shakespeare uses this dialogue to show the mental turmoil that the pursuit of power has caused. Ironically, the Macbeths seem powerless and are at the mercy of the witches' words and the perceived threats of Banquo and Macduff.
'I will tomorrow— And betimes I will—to the weïrd sisters. More shall they speak. For now I am bent to know By the worst means, the worst;' (Act 3 Scene 4)	This dialogue reveals how a powerful king is at the mercy of the witches, a group of socially powerless women. Determining his future plans on the predictions of the witches suggests he is not a rational or fit king.
'What's more to do Which would be planted newly with the time,— As calling home our exil'd friends abroad That fled the snares of watchful tyranny,' (Act 5 Scene 9)	Malcolm's speech in the play's resolution suggests he will use his power wisely to welcome back the thanes who deserted Scotland under Macbeth's reign. It shows that he will use his reign to heal Scotland and restore order and harmony. It also confirms that Macbeth was viewed as a tyrant.

Five key points about power

1. A ruthless desire for power and status leads to immoral actions.
2. Power is achieved, maintained, and lost through violent actions.
3. Good kingship is linked to moral choices that are selfless.
4. Words and suggestions can have a very powerful influence.
5. Powerful kings can be controlled by apparently powerless characters.

> **REVISION TIP**
>
> Track the loss and gain of power for the main characters in the play. Look at which characters Shakespeare gives power to by the end of the play and consider what moral message this creates.

14

Writing about power

Sample answer 1: not a strong answer

Here is an extract from a student response to this question, with the examiner's annotations and final comments. It receives less than half marks.

> How does Shakespeare present kingship?
>
> [30 marks]
> AO4 [4 marks]

❶ A simple and relevant comment

> There are three kings in the play – Duncan, Macbeth, and Malcolm – and they all act in different ways. ❶ Duncan is a good king who gives out titles and is well thought of. Macbeth is a cruel king who murders his enemies. Malcolm will be a better king and should have been on the throne in the first place. ❷ Shakespeare uses these contrasting kings to make a big point about kingship. ❸

❷ These descriptions are accurate but not developed.

❸ There is a sense of the writer's method here, but the comment is vague.

Examiner's comments

Relevant and accurate points about three kings are made, but they are simple rather than developed. There is an awareness of the writer's method.

REMEMBER

Avoid empty, generalised phrases such as 'Shakespeare makes a big point about kingship'. They say very little. Instead, clearly define the point you are making. For instance, in this sample answer, a more specific point might be: 'Shakespeare suggests that the moral values of Malcolm and Duncan make them far more suitable kings than Macbeth.'

Knowledge

Knowledge — THEMES

14 Power

Sample answer 2: a strong answer

Here is an extract from a student response to this question, with the examiner's annotations and final comments. It receives high marks.

> How does Shakespeare present kingship?
>
> [30 marks]
> AO4 [4 marks]

① A good awareness of structural choices linked to meanings

> Shakespeare chooses to end the play with Malcolm's speech, resolving the narrative with a return to order after the chaos of Macbeth's rule. ① The final speech signifies a more stately and honourable type of kingship. Not only does Malcolm promise to repay his supporters, he extends powers to the thanes who will 'Henceforth be earls', and welcomes back exiled Scots. This compares favourably to Macbeth's reign, where thanes were sidelined and the king was a 'butcher' rather than a benevolent ruler. ② Shakespeare suggests that good kingship means acting morally and inclusively for the good of all. ③

② Effective detail from the text showing the contrast between kings

③ A perceptive comment on what is being shown about kingship

Examiner's comments

A fluent and thoughtful response that sees how Shakespeare's choices make meanings. There are some perceptive points being made about kingship here.

REVISION TIP

There are times when you need to use precise and sometimes complex terms to express complex ideas. It is usually the case that an excellent response will be written in fluent prose. Use some of the responses in this book to widen your vocabulary.

Key terms — Make sure you can write a definition for these key terms

characterise   simile

14 Power

Retrieval 14

Answer the questions below. Cover the answers column with a piece of paper and write down as many answers as you can. Check and repeat.

Questions / Answers

#	Questions	Answers
1	Many themes and ideas in the play overlap. True or false?	True
2	Describe how Duncan acts as king.	He uses his power thoughtfully and rewards loyalty
3	Lady Macbeth needs no help to achieve power. True or false?	False. She requests the aid of dark forces
4	Describe how Macbeth acts as king.	He abuses his power and maintains it through murder
5	Describe how Malcolm acts as king.	He appears to have the makings of a good king, who will use his power wisely
6	What method is used in the line 'his virtues Will plead like angels'?	Simile
7	What does the line 'his virtues Will plead like angels' suggest about Duncan?	God is on his side
8	Give three key points about power shown in the play.	Three from: A ruthless desire for power and status leads to immoral actions / Power is achieved, maintained, and lost through violent actions / Good kingship is linked to moral choices that are selfless / Words and suggestions can have a very powerful influence / Powerful kings can be controlled by apparently powerless characters
9	Complete the quotation using two words. 'Better _____ the dead'	'Better <u>be with</u> the dead'
10	Complete the quotation. 'As calling home our exil'd _____ abroad That fled the snares of watchful _____,'	'As calling home our exil'd <u>friends</u> abroad That fled the snares of watchful <u>tyranny</u>,'

Previous questions

Now go back and use these questions to check your knowledge of previous topics.

#	Questions	Answers
1	Whose words awaken Macbeth's ambitions?	The witches'
2	Macbeth's ambitions cause unhappiness. True or false?	True
3	Describe Macduff's ambitions.	A selfless ambition to help Scotland get rid of Macbeth
4	What method is used in the phrase 'vaulting ambition'?	Metaphor

Now turn to page 106 and complete Practice question 9.

Knowledge — THEMES

15 Death and violence

Death and violence

Several deaths occur in the play, often with different functions. Violence is shown as a way to gain and maintain power – the world of the play is a violent one.

Key events involving death and violence

- A violent battle for control of Scotland occurs as the play opens.
- Macbeth uses extreme violence on the battlefield to defend Duncan's rule.
- Duncan has the rebellious original Thane of Cawdor executed.
- Macbeth murders Duncan to gain power and murders his chamberlains to silence them.
- Macbeth arranges the murder of Banquo and Fleance to protect his position.
- Macbeth arranges the murder of Macduff's family as punishment for Macduff's departure for England and the threat he poses.
- Lady Macbeth kills herself – a tragic consequence of her actions.
- Malcolm and Macduff lead a violent assault on Macbeth's castle.
- Macbeth kills young Siward, thinking himself invulnerable to attack.
- Macduff kills Macbeth, and order is restored to Scotland.

REVISION TIP

As well as thinking about the meanings of events, also consider the function of them. For example, Macbeth's death has the function of restoring order.

15

Five key lines about death and violence

Lines	What they show about death and violence
'So well thy words become thee as thy wounds; They smack of honour both. Go, get him surgeons'. (Act 1 Scene 2, said by Duncan to a soldier)	This dialogue is used to establish the world of the text and its values. In it, violence is associated with honour and power – it suggests 'good' men are loyal and prepared to fight.
'Here lay Duncan, His silver skin lac'd with his golden blood And his gash'd stabs look'd like a breach in nature,' (Act 2 Scene 3)	Macbeth's dialogue recounts the violence shown to Duncan in imagery of precious metals. Dramatic irony allows the audience to know that he is guilty, but his words also suggest his remorse and horror at his actions.
'And with him, To leave no rubs nor botches in the work, Fleance, his son that keeps him company, Whose absence is no less material to me Than is his father's,' (Act 3 Scene 1)	Shakespeare uses Macbeth's dialogue to show how his attitude to murder has changed, as here he shows no sign of conscience. The figurative use of 'work' shows that he regards the murders as simply a job to be done.
'The time has been That when the brains were out, the man would die, And there an end. But now they rise again' (Act 3 Scene 4)	Macbeth's words about the appearance of Banquo's ghost implies that murder cannot put an end to Macbeth's misery. The symbol of the ghost suggests that consequences are inescapable and past acts must be confronted.
Enter Macduff, *with Macbeth's head* 'Hail, king, for so thou art. Behold where stands Th'usurper's cursed head. The time is free.' (Act 5 Scene 9)	The stage direction suggests the dramatic nature of Macbeth's end and acts as a symbol of punishment. His death signifies a return to order and the end of chaos.

Five key points about death and violence

1. The world of the text is one where violence is linked to masculinity.
2. Death and violence are ways of achieving power.
3. Death and violence are methods of control and revenge.
4. Both innocent and guilty characters die during the play.
5. Death is a way of restoring order at the end of the tragedy.

REVISION TIP

Look carefully at the moral ideas emerging from death and violence. Some deaths seem to be justified as a form of punishment.

Knowledge — THEMES

15 Death and violence

Writing about death and violence

Sample answer 1: not a strong answer

Here is an extract from a student response to this question, with the examiner's annotations and final comments. It receives less than half marks.

> How does Shakespeare present ideas about death in the play?
>
> [30 marks]
> AO4 [4 marks]

> At the start of the play, Macbeth kills on the battlefield and 'unseams' a rebel. This is seen as good, and he is rewarded for it. ❶ However, he knows that killing Duncan is wrong, which is why he spends a lot of time debating it. I think there is a difference between killing in a war and murdering a king who doesn't deserve it. ❷ You can see that he regrets it straight away. He hears knocking and thinks his hands are covered in blood. ❸

❶ A relevant reference with a straightforward comment

❷ Another straightforward comment, which would have benefited from development

❸ A useful reference, but little sense of its wider meaning or the method used

Examiner's comments

Question focus is good here, but the ideas and comments are only straightforward rather than thoughtful. There is no real awareness of Shakespeare's methods.

REMEMBER

Choosing which examples to write about is a key exam skill. Assuming you know the text well, there may be several scenes or events you could write about in an answer. Always spend time working out which ones would be best – which ones you could say most about and explore.

15

Sample answer 2: a strong answer

Here is an extract from a student response to this question, with the examiner's annotations and final comments. It receives high marks.

> How far does Shakespeare present ideas about death in the play?
>
> [30 marks]
> AO4 [4 marks]

❶ A perceptive point with a sense of how a relevant method is used

Shakespeare contrasts supposedly legitimate deaths with ones that have less moral justification. ❶ In the early phase of the play, it is reported that Macbeth violently 'unseams' a rebel and is then rewarded by Duncan. This implies that such deaths are acceptable when they are in defence of the status quo. Likewise, closing the play with the death of Macbeth brings an end to his cruel reign and signifies order being restored. ❷ These events are shown to be acceptable as they are in the wider public interest. Other deaths are much more selfish in nature. For example, Banquo's murder is simply about Macbeth protecting his own power. ❸

❷ Specific examples with perceptive comments

❸ This develops the point set up earlier with further perceptive thought.

Examiner's comments

Insightful comments are made, which show a range of ideas and references. The response is fluently written and explores how the playwright uses structure to make meaning.

REVISION TIP

Spend time reading a range of high-quality student responses. As well as the ones in this book, explore the material on AQA's website. Your teacher may have access to other resources to help you develop your skills as you revise.

Knowledge

Retrieval

Answer the questions below. Cover the answers column with a piece of paper and write down as many answers as you can. Check and repeat.

Questions

1. Macbeth uses extreme violence on the battlefield. True or false?
2. Macbeth murders Duncan's chamberlains to silence them. True or false?
3. Explain why Macbeth has Banquo murdered.
4. Explain why Macbeth has Macduff's family murdered.
5. Complete the quotation. 'So well thy words become thee as thy _____; They smack of _____ both.'
6. Name a method used in the line 'His silver skin lac'd with his golden blood'?
7. What does the line 'His silver skin lac'd with his golden blood' suggest about Duncan?
8. Both Macbeth and Lady Macbeth die in the final act of the play. True or false?
9. Complete the quotation. 'The time has been That when the ____ were out, the man would ___;'
10. Give three key points about death and violence shown in the play.

Answers

1. True
2. True
3. To protect his position
4. Punishment for Macduff's threat
5. 'So well thy words become thee as thy <u>wounds</u>; They smack of <u>honour</u> both.'
6. One from: Imagery / Dramatic irony
7. It associates Duncan with items of value, suggesting his worth as a man and a king
8. True
9. 'The time has been That when the <u>brains</u> were out, the man would <u>die</u>,'
10. Three from: Violence is linked to masculinity / Death and violence are ways of achieving power / They are methods of control and revenge / Both innocent and guilty characters die / Death is a way of restoring order at the end

Previous questions

Now go back and use these questions to check your knowledge of previous topics.

Questions

1. What method is used in the line 'his virtues / Will plead like angels'?
2. Complete the quotation using two words: 'Better _____ the dead'

Answers

1. Simile
2. 'Better <u>be with</u> the dead'

Now turn to page 107 and complete Practice question 10.

15 Death and violence

Knowledge — THEMES — 16

16 Deception

Deception

'Deception' means making someone believe something that isn't true. Many characters in the play deceive each other, usually to gain power. Some characters allow themselves to be deceived. The term 'deception' covers ideas about lying, disloyalty, manipulation, and appearance versus reality.

> **REVISION TIP**
> Explore which characters are deceivers and which are deceived. Consider how closely this is linked to their moral goodness.

Key events involving deception

- *Banquo warns Macbeth not to be tricked by the witches' words.*
- Macbeth's desire for power makes him blind to the witches' intentions – he allows himself to be deceived.
- Lady Macbeth advises her husband to conceal his true intentions more.
- Lady Macbeth deceives herself into thinking she can avoid guilt and consequences.
- The Macbeths deceive Duncan while planning his murder.
- The Macbeths pretend they are innocent of Duncan's murder.
- Macbeth manipulates the murderers into killing Banquo.
- Macbeth maintains a friendship with Banquo while planning his death.
- Macbeth is deceived a second time by the witches' apparent assurances about his future.
- *Malcolm and Macduff aren't deceived by Macbeth's lies.*
- Macbeth realises too late that he has been deceived by the witches.
- *Malcolm appears to be a more honest and trustworthy king.*

> **REVISION TIP**
> Spend time thinking closely about Macbeth's self-deception. Is he completely unaware that he is being played by the witches, or does he have an awareness of their trickery?

> **REMEMBER**
> Many of the ideas and themes in *Macbeth* seem to have negative, immoral associations. Be prepared to think in a more nuanced way about some of them. For instance, the approaching soldiers initially deceive Macbeth with their camouflage – is the audience encouraged to see this as a positive thing, given that they are seen as being on the 'right' side of the conflict? Considering matters in such ways often leads to perceptive thoughts.

Knowledge  THEMES

16 Deception

Five key lines about deception

Lines	What they show about deception
'And oftentimes, to win us to our harm, / The instruments of darkness tell us truths; / Win us with honest trifles, to betray's / In deepest consequence.' (Act 1 Scene 3)	Banquo's dialogue sets up a contrast between his scepticism about the witches' trustworthiness and Macbeth's attitude towards the witches. This tragic warning is ignored and shows how Macbeth's ambition blinds him to deception.
'look like th'innocent flower, / But be the serpent under't.' (Act 1 Scene 5)	Shakespeare uses these images of innocence and evil to show Lady Macbeth's conscious attempt to deceive. The serpent image links deception to evil.
'There's no art / To find the mind's construction in the face. / He was a gentleman on whom I built / An absolute trust.' (Act 1 Scene 4)	Duncan's lines about the original Thane of Cawdor show that he realises appearances can't always be trusted. Ironically, he repeats the same mistake with the Macbeths.
'Stars, hide your fires, / Let not light see my black and deep desires,' (Act 1 Scene 4)	The dark imagery in Macbeth's lines suggest he knows that deception is an evil act that needs to be concealed.
'Where we are, / There's daggers in men's smiles;' (Act 2 Scene 3)	Donaldbain's dialogue with Malcolm contrasts imagery of threat and trustworthiness. It suggests that some characters aren't as easily deceived by other's pretences.

Five key points about deception

1. A desire for power causes characters to deceive others.
2. Those who choose to deceive are morally corrupt.
3. Deceit leads to loss of sanity, suffering, and death for the deceivers.
4. People can be very different to how they superficially appear.
5. Honesty is linked to moral goodness.

REVISION TIP

Look at how Shakespeare places ideas about deception in the play's structure. Explore how he shows initial deceptions and how these lies unravel later in the story.

REMEMBER

Some ideas in the text (such as Lady Macbeth's reference to the 'serpent' in Act 1 Scene 4) refer to other texts, such as the Bible. You don't need to spend time explaining where the reference comes from. Assume your examiner knows and spend time exploring the meanings of such ideas.

16

Writing about deception

Sample answer 1: not a strong answer

Here is an extract from a student response to this question, with the examiner's annotations and final comments. It receives less than half marks.

> How does Shakespeare present ideas about lies and deception?
>
> [30 marks]
> AO4 [4 marks]

① A useful reference with a straightforward comment

Lady Macbeth tells her husband to 'look like th'innocent flower, But be the serpent under't', which means conceal your bad thoughts by looking innocent. This shows that she knows what they're going to do is wrong. ① This makes her seem a terrible person, because she cunningly plans the murder and goes ahead even though they shouldn't. ② Macbeth knows that he needs to conceal his bad thoughts. When Malcolm is announced as the next king by Duncan, Macbeth struggles to keep his reaction hidden, saying 'Let not light see my black and deep desires'. ③

② A good point that needs more development

③ Another relevant point, but needs a better supporting comment and sense of method

Examiner's comments

Relevant points and references are made with a competent understanding. Comments are straightforward and there is little sense of method.

REVISION TIP

Make sure you don't 'over-quote' – don't litter your work with lots of quotations. Instead, when you do choose to use a quotation, select precise words from the text that help make your point.

REMEMBER

You don't get marks for the number of quotations you use. You get marks for the quality of your comments and argument. You may use quotations or references, but only use them when they are directly relevant to the point being made.

Knowledge 73

Knowledge — THEMES

16 Deception

Sample answer 2: a strong answer

Here is an extract from a student response to this question, with the examiner's annotations and final comments. It receives high marks.

> How does Shakespeare present ideas about lies and deception?
>
> [30 marks]
> AO4 [4 marks]

① A thoughtful point that sees how structural choices help meanings to emerge

Shakespeare structures events to show how most attempts to deceive are motivated by a selfish desire for power. ① By the resolution of the story, those who deceive are punished for their actions (with the exception of the witches), and so a moral message emerges: liars will be punished in the end. ② Lady Macbeth's advice to Macbeth to be an 'innocent flower' proves ironically unhelpful for herself as she suffers mental turmoil. Macbeth's own attempts at deception are initially successful, but he fails to fully see that he himself is being deceived by the cryptic words of the witches. His desire to believe them suggests that his ambitions blind him to their trickery. ③

② Another perceptive point that gets to the heart of what is being shown about deception

③ This point uses a well-chosen example to neatly link the big ideas of the text.

Examiner's comments

A perceptive series of points that show how methods are used to make big points about morality. The response is fluently written and thoughtful throughout.

REMEMBER

Literary works are written in order to say something about life and human conduct. *Macbeth* explores these issues and presents moral views about them. Perceptive writing often explores these higher-order ideas that emerge in the play.

REVISION TIP

One way to develop your higher-order thinking as you revise is to ask yourself, 'What moral message is being given about this event, character, or theme?' Exploring the text in this way will encourage you to write more conceptual and more successful responses.

Retrieval

16

Answer the questions below. Cover the answers column with a piece of paper and write down as many answers as you can. Check and repeat.

Questions | Answers

#	Question	Answer
1	Who warns Macbeth not to be tricked by the witches' words?	Banquo
2	Macbeth advises Lady Macbeth to conceal her true intentions. True or false?	False (it's the other way around)
3	Macbeth maintains a friendship with Banquo while planning his death. True or false?	True
4	Which two characters are not deceived by the Macbeths?	Malcolm and Macduff
5	Who appears to be a more honest and trustworthy king – Macbeth or Malcolm?	Malcolm
6	Complete the quotation. 'Win us with _____ trifles, to _____ In deepest consequence.'	'Win us with honest trifles, to betray's In deepest consequence.'
7	What method is used in this quotation? 'look like th'innocent flower, But be the serpent under't.'	Imagery
8	What does 'look like th'innocent flower, But be the serpent under't' suggest about Lady Macbeth?	That she is deceptive and evil
9	Complete the quotation. 'There's no art To find the _____ construction in the _____.'	'There's no art To find the mind's construction in the face.'
10	Give three key points about deception shown in the play.	Three from: A desire for power causes characters to deceive others / Those who choose to deceive are morally corrupt / Deceit leads to loss of sanity, suffering, and death / People can be very different to how they appear / Honesty is linked to moral goodness

Previous questions

Now go back and use these questions to check your knowledge of previous topics.

Questions | Answers

#	Question	Answer
1	Describe Lady Macbeth's ambitions.	She desires the power that would result from her husband becoming king
2	Describe how Duncan acts as king.	He uses his power thoughtfully and rewards loyalty
3	Explain why Macbeth has Banquo murdered.	To protect his position

Now turn to page 109 and complete Practice question 12.

Knowledge — THEMES

17 Suffering and guilt

Suffering and guilt

Suffering and guilt are the effects of tragic errors. Although some innocent characters suffer, guilty characters are shown to receive punishment for their actions in the end.

Key events involving suffering and guilt

- Duncan and his sons are innocent characters who suffer as a result of Macbeth's ambitions.
- Macbeth is given glimpses and warnings of future suffering and guilt, but ignores them.
- Macbeth feels guilt and remorse immediately after murdering Duncan.
- Lady Macbeth initially assumes she can avoid feeling any guilt.
- The witches' prediction about Banquo's sons torments Macbeth.
- Lady Macbeth secretly confesses to feeling despair.
- Macbeth is tormented by lack of sleep and insecurity.
- Banquo and the Macduffs are innocents who are made to suffer for Macbeth's cruelty.
- Macbeth gradually feels less remorse.
- Lady Macbeth suffers mental turmoil as a result of her actions and dies.
- Macbeth is forced to face what he has become – a tragic realisation of his actions.
- The suffering of Scotland is brought to an end by Macbeth's death.

REVISION TIP
Themes develop and take on extra layers as a story progresses. As you revise, explore how Macbeth's suffering changes during the course of the play, and what this might suggest about the experience of being a murderer does to humans.

REMEMBER
Suffering and guilt are classic effects of a tragic decision – one that brings misery. When you write about ideas and themes that allow you to naturally connect with the concept of tragedy, then do so.

17 Suffering and guilt

Five key lines about suffering and guilt

Lines	What they show about suffering and guilt
'Methought I heard a voice cry, "Sleep no more: Macbeth does murder sleep", the innocent sleep,' (Act 2 Scene 2)	This dialogue suggests the immediate guilt felt by Macbeth in the early part of the play, suggesting he has some moral scruples at this point. The figurative use of 'innocent' suggests that Macbeth realises he has committed a terrible and evil act.
'A little water clears us of this deed. How easy is it then!' (Act 2 Scene 2)	Lady Macbeth's dialogue suggests that at this point in the play, she believes guilt can figuratively be washed away. This contrasts with her later tragic suffering.
'O, full of scorpions is my mind, dear wife!' (Act 3 Scene 2)	This use of figurative language in Macbeth's dialogue suggests the torment he feels – perhaps indicating he feels scared and overrun with his mental terrors.
'But now I am cabin'd, cribb'd, confin'd, bound in To saucy doubts and fears'. (Act 3 Scene 4)	The appearance of Banquo's ghost prompts Macbeth to declare his terror at the symbolic reminder of his guilt. The figurative language shows how he feels trapped by what he has done.
'And that which should accompany old age, As honour, love, obedience, troops of friends, I must not look to have;' (Act 5 Scene 3)	Shakespeare structures the play to show that, by the end of the tragic journey, Macbeth comes to realise that his actions have left him loveless and friendless, showing that terrible actions have consequences for the perpetrator.

Five key points about suffering and guilt

1. Reckless ambition and cruel acts cause suffering to innocent people.
2. Those who transgress normal behaviour experience suffering and guilt as a consequence.
3. Tragic characters are made to confront their suffering and guilt.
4. Suffering and guilt have a moral dimension, with some characters deserving their turmoil.
5. Suffering often culminates in death as a type of tragic release.

> **REVISION TIP**
>
> Remember that ideas about suffering and guilt can be seen as part of a character's tragic journey. Look closely at passages where characters reflect on their feelings, suggesting their tragic realisation of what they have become.

Knowledge — THEMES

17 Suffering and guilt

Writing about suffering and guilt

Sample answer 1: not a strong answer

Here is an extract from a student response to this question, with the examiner's annotations and final comments. It receives less than half marks.

> How far does Shakespeare present Macbeth as a character who suffers?
>
> [30 marks]
> AO4 [4 marks]

> Macbeth is a character who suffers. He does terrible things and then pays for it. For instance, he thinks he hears voices. He also sees Banquo's ghost. ❶ Macbeth suffers a lot and feels plenty of guilt because of the crimes he did. He feels bad about killing Duncan. He feels less bad about killing Banquo. This shows that he changes. ❷ Overall, Macbeth is a character who suffers and he deserves it. ❸

❶ Relevant point here with straightforward comment

❷ This is a good idea, which needs developing

❸ A brief concluding comment that would have benefited from further explanation

Examiner's comments

The points made here are all relevant, but they need better explanation and further supporting comments from the student. Useful references are given, and there is a basic sense of structural choices.

REVISION TIP

Sometimes 'writing a bit more' can help your work – push yourself to extend and develop the comments you make. It's hard to write a good response if you write underdeveloped points.

REMEMBER

Some exam questions invite a debate around a character. You must give a view on the debate set up in the question, but there is no need to produce a 'for-and-against' response. You are free to agree or disagree entirely with the prompt. You can learn more about response structure on page 88.

Sample answer 2: a strong answer

Here is an extract from a student response to this question, with the examiner's annotations and final comments. It receives high marks.

> How far does Shakespeare present Macbeth as a character who suffers?
>
> **[30 marks]**
> **AO4 [4 marks]**

❶ Well-phrased with relevant and specific references

Macbeth's mental anguish begins almost immediately. He hears knocking sounds, thinks he hears a voice telling him he will 'sleep no more' and is frightened to look upon what he has done. ❶ The structural placement of his suffering next to the act of murder helps to make the point that actions have consequences. It does seem that, once he has killed Duncan, he is never happy again, observing 'Better be with the dead'. ❷ Macbeth's suffering is also expressed in a range of animal metaphors: his mind is 'full of scorpions'. This animal image suggests that his suffering and fear are, like animals, uncontrollable and potentially deadly. ❸

❷ A good awareness of structure, with another specific and well-chosen reference

❸ A perceptive comment on how figurative language expresses meaning

Examiner's comments

Several insightful comments are made using specific and well-chosen references. There is a good awareness of how structural choices create meaning.

REVISION TIP

Make sure that, when you comment on a specific quotation, you do so in the context of the play. For instance, Macbeth's line about his mind being 'full of scorpions' can be explored in the context of his turmoil at that particular stage of the play. Never be drawn into speculation about events that aren't shown or referenced in the play. Don't try to imagine a backstory for Macbeth's mental turmoil that isn't supported by what is shown in the text.

REMEMBER

It's often better to write about structural methods that lead you naturally to explore ideas, but when you choose to focus on smaller aspects of method, figurative language can often be a very effective area.

Knowledge 79

Retrieval

Answer the questions below. Cover the answers column with a piece of paper and write down as many answers as you can. Check and repeat.

Questions | Answers

#	Question	Answer
1	Name two innocent characters who suffer.	Two from: Duncan / Banquo / Fleance / Malcolm / Donaldbain / the Macduff family / Young Siward
2	Macbeth feels little guilt or remorse straight after murdering Duncan. True or false?	False
3	Lady Macbeth secretly confesses to feeling despair. True or false?	True
4	Describe how Macbeth's feelings of guilt change during the play.	Macbeth gradually feels less remorse
5	Describe how Lady Macbeth suffers in the final act of the play.	She suffers mental turmoil as a result of her actions and dies
6	Complete the quotation using three words. 'As _____, troops of friends, I must not look to have'	'As <u>honour, love, obedience</u>, troops of friends, I must not look to have'
7	What method is used in the line: 'O, full of scorpions is my mind, dear wife!'?	Figurative language
8	What does the line 'full of scorpions is my mind' show about Macbeth's feelings of torment?	He feels scared and overrun with his mental terrors
9	Complete the quotation. 'But now I am _____, cribb'd, _____, bound in'	'But now I am <u>cabin'd</u>, cribb'd, <u>confin'd</u>, bound in'
10	Give three key points about suffering and guilt shown in the play.	Three from: Reckless ambition and cruel acts cause suffering to the innocent / Those who transgress normal behaviour experience suffering and guilt as a consequence / Tragic characters are made to confront their suffering and guilt / Suffering and guilt have a moral dimension, with some characters deserving their turmoil / Suffering often culminates in death as a type of tragic release

Previous questions

Now go back and use these questions to check your knowledge of previous topics.

Questions | Answers

#	Question	Answer
1	Lady Macbeth needs no help to achieve power. True or false?	False. She requests the aid of dark forces
2	Macbeth murders Duncan's chamberlains to silence them. True or false?	True
3	Who warns Macbeth not to be tricked by the witches' words?	Banquo

Now turn to page 110 and complete Practice question 13.

17 Suffering and guilt

Knowledge

THEMES

18 Evil and the supernatural

Evil and the supernatural

Evil is a moral concept, which suggests cruelty and terrible beliefs and behaviours. Characters, both 'real' and supernatural, can act in (and be drawn into) evil ways.

Key events involving evil and the supernatural

- The witches offer predictions about Macbeth's future that awaken his ambition.
- Macbeth is warned about the dangers of trusting the words of supernatural beings, but ignores this.
- Lady Macbeth requests help from dark forces to bring about the death of Duncan.
- Macbeth sees a floating dagger leading him towards Duncan.
- Macbeth and Lady Macbeth give in to their evil ambitions and kill Duncan.
- Macbeth realises that his evil actions have corrupted and harmed him.
- Lady Macbeth doesn't feel that her actions are evil or potentially harmful to herself.
- Banquo's ghost appears to Macbeth – a reminder of his evil acts and guilt.
- The witches give a second set of predictions to Macbeth, which he foolishly trusts.
- Macbeth arranges the evil act of killing the innocent Macduff family.
- The Macbeths suffer and die – punishment for their evil actions
- The witches remain unpunished for their influence over Macbeth.

Knowledge

THEMES

18 Evil and the supernatural

Five key lines about evil and the supernatural

Lines	What they show about evil and the supernatural
'My noble partner You greet with present grace and great prediction Of noble having and of royal hope That he seems rapt withal.' (Act 1 Scene 3)	Banquo's dialogue with the witches is used to reveal Macbeth's reaction to the predictions – he is spellbound. This suggests that he is quickly seduced by their words as they chime with his ambitions.
'Come, thick night, And pall thee in the dunnest smoke of hell, That my keen knife see not the wound it makes' (Act 1 Scene 5)	Shakespeare uses this soliloquy to show how easily Lady Macbeth allows evil to take hold. The images of violence and concealment emphasise the terrifying nature of evil.
'What cannot you and I perform upon Th' unguarded Duncan? What not put upon His spongy officers, who shall bear the guilt' (Act 1 Scene 7)	This dialogue shows how comfortable Lady Macbeth is with evil: she sees murder as a performance and shows no worries about laying the blame upon innocent guards.
'I would, while it was smiling in my face, Have pluck'd my nipple from his boneless gums And dash'd the brains out,' (Act 1 Scene 7)	The use of this violent image reinforces Lady Macbeth's evil qualities. The phrase contrasts an image of innocence with that of evil, suggesting that evil is a terrifying, immoral quality.
'I am in blood Stepp'd in so far that should I wade no more, Returning were as tedious as go o'er.' (Act 3 Scene 4)	This figurative language suggests that once Macbeth has committed an evil act, it is inevitable that he continues. It reveals that evil becomes commonplace to him.

Five key points about evil and the supernatural

1. A desire for power causes characters to commit evil acts.
2. Evil acts result in temporary triumph, but ultimate defeat.
3. Evil powers are deceptive and have a tragic influence.
4. Supernatural events can symbolise human emotions.
5. Evil acts cause the perpetrators to lose their humanity.

> **REVISION TIP**
>
> Consider how writers use contrast to highlight ideas. For example, evil acts become much more striking when placed against images of innocence.

> **REMEMBER**
>
> 'The supernatural' includes the witches, Hecate, Banquo's ghost, and the various apparitions.
>
> It is debatable whether the dagger Macbeth sees in Act 2 Scene 1 is a supernatural entity or simply (as he thinks) a product of his mind. Some film interpretations present it as a supernatural entity. If you choose to write about it as such, briefly state so. A useful phrase might be: 'It is possible to interpret the dagger as a supernatural entity…'

18

Writing about evil and the supernatural

Sample answer 1: not a strong answer

Here is an extract from a student response to this question, with the examiner's annotations and final comments. It receives less than half marks.

> How does Shakespeare present ideas about evil in *Macbeth*?
>
> [30 marks]
> AO4 [4 marks]

❶ Relevant examples here, but little comment

❷ There is a competent understanding, but the reference isn't clearly explained.

❸ Another competent point that would have benefited from further explanation

There are lots of evil acts in 'Macbeth'. For instance, the Macbeths kill Duncan, Banquo, and the Macduffs. ❶ These show that evil is linked to death and that evil actions are about people using their power wrongly – Lady Macbeth uses the phrase 'dash'd the brains out'. ❷ At the end of the play, the people who are evil are all punished. Both Macbeth and his wife die. This shows that evil doesn't pay and that bad people never prosper. ❸

Examiner's comments

The points made here are relevant and competent, but underexplained. There is a vague sense of the writer's method, but it's not explained clearly.

REVISION TIP

Always check the last parts of each paragraph when your re-read your work. It's usually these parts where you are developing a point and making a comment. Ask yourself how much effort has gone into this aspect of your work. If your exploratory comments are thin (as in Sample answer 1), extend them.

REMEMBER

It is better to make thoughtful and detailed points about obvious examples than to pick obscure parts of the text, or argue odd or illogical points. For instance, trying to argue that Macduff's killing of Macbeth is evil is possible but hard to do. Sometimes these types of off-kilter views can fall flat rather than appear impressive.

Knowledge

Knowledge — THEMES

18 Evil and the supernatural

Sample answer 2: a strong answer

Here is an extract from a student response to this question, with the examiner's annotations and final comments. It receives high marks.

> How does Shakespeare present ideas about evil in *Macbeth*?
>
> [30 marks]
> AO4 [4 marks]

① A perceptive point that shows how structure is used to make a thematic point

> The structure of the play is an exploration of how evil operates. It shows how a loyal, good man descends into evil, and how his actions destroy not only the lives of those around him, but his own too. ① The audience is shown the journey of the central character, which ends in his tragic downfall, emphasising a key moral message: that evil actions will ultimately result in punishment and death. ② By the resolution of the narrative, the audience is shown how engaging with evil causes people to lose their compassion and ultimately lose everything. ③

② Another perceptive point that gets to the heart of what message is being given about evil

③ Another perceptive point about how structural choices create meaning

Examiner's comments

There is a very insightful grasp on the moral messages that arise from evil acts. The student can clearly see how Shakespeare's structural choices reveal these messages.

REVISION TIP

Make an effort to note down phrases and words that express difficult concepts and ideas. Often, these phrases and words are complex in themselves, but don't avoid them. Instead, make a conscious effort to become confident with them, and use them precisely in your own writing where they are needed.

REMEMBER

Being 'perceptive' means showing off your high-quality thinking. You can only do this when you have mastered the details of the text and spent time thinking about the ideas and moral messages that emerge. See 'being perceptive' as something you can do when you know details and can stand back from the play and see the wider points it is making.

Retrieval 18

Answer the questions below. Cover the answers column with a piece of paper and write down as many answers as you can. Check and repeat.

Questions | Answers

1. Which character asks for help from dark forces? — Lady Macbeth
2. Macbeth realises that his evil actions have corrupted and harmed him. True or false? — True
3. Lady Macbeth thinks her husband should be more evil to achieve his ambitions. True or false? — True
4. Explain what Banquo's ghost symbolises. — A reminder of Macbeth's evil intentions and guilt
5. Describe the Macbeths' punishment for their evil actions. — They suffer and die
6. What method is used in the line 'Come, thick night, And pall thee in the dunnest smoke of hell'? — Imagery
7. What does the line 'pall thee in the dunnest smoke of hell' suggest about evil? — Its terrifying nature
8. Give three key points about evil and supernatural shown in the play. — Three from: A desire for power causes characters to commit evil acts / Evil acts result in temporary triumph, but ultimate defeat / Evil powers are deceptive and have a tragic influence / Supernatural events can symbolise human emotions / Evil acts cause the perpetrators to lose their humanity
9. Complete the quotation using three words. 'What not put upon His spongy officers who shall _____.' — 'What not put upon His spongy officers who shall <u>bear the guilt</u>.'
10. Complete the quotation. 'I am in _____ Stepp'd in so far that should I _____ no more,' — 'I am in <u>blood</u> Stepp'd in so far that should I <u>wade</u> no more,'

Previous questions

Now go back and use these questions to check your knowledge of previous topics.

Questions | Answers

1. Explain why Macbeth has Macduff's family murdered. — Punishment for Macduff's threat
2. Macbeth advises Lady Macbeth to conceal her true intentions. True or false? — False. It's the other way around
3. Lady Macbeth secretly confesses to feeling despair. True or false? — True

> Now turn to page 112 and complete Practice question 15.

Knowledge **EXAM SKILLS**

Exam skills

Exam skills

You must know the text well to write a successful exam response. Make sure you are familiar with the plot, method, character, and ideas before attempting this and the next section.

> **EXAM TIP**
> The best source of advice about the exam is the examiner's reports on AQA's website – these are written by the people who set papers and mark responses.

Key exam paper information

- The *Macbeth* question is in Paper 1 Section A. You are marked out of 30 (plus 4 marks for AO4).
- You will spend roughly 50 minutes answering it.
- You will be given a question and reminder points.
- Your response must refer to the printed extract.
- You must also refer to events in the rest of the play.

Assessment objectives

① AO1: the quality of your response and understanding and use of the text

This includes the style and way in which you write, and how you use references and quotations.

There is no link between the number of quotations you use and your mark. It is possible to write an excellent response using a few quotations or references – it's your ideas that are important. So don't spend all of your revision time learning lots of quotations. Revise characters and ideas.

② AO2: your understanding of the writer's methods

This means grasping how the structure and language choices used help to show ideas. You should use appropriate terms where needed.

You do not need to refer to complex techniques and terms to do well. The point you make and the quality of your comment are more important. Use terms such as the ones seen in this book, like resolution, metaphor, dialogue.

③ AO3: your understanding of ideas and contexts

This is about showing how well you understand the ideas and meanings in the play.

There is no need to write about historical context – usually it gets in the way of a good answer. Writing about the ideas of the text is how you address AO3.

④ AO4: your phrasing and technical accuracy

This means how clear and accurate your writing is.

It is better to write clearly and directly in exams. Don't tie yourself in knots trying to 'show off' elaborate phrasing.

Types of question

Questions are typically set up in one of two ways:

Explore how Shakespeare presents… → Invited to explore an idea

Explore how far Shakespeare presents… → Invited to offer a view

> **LINK**
> You can see examples of different types of questions on pages 108–112.

These questions give an opportunity to show off your knowledge of the text, its ideas, and the quality of your understanding.

86 Exam skills

A sample exam question

Read the following extract from Act 5 Scene 5 ❶ of *Macbeth* and then answer the question.

❶ This tells you where the extract comes from in the play.

- At this point in the play, Lady Macbeth has just killed herself, and Macbeth is preparing for his castle to be attacked. ❷

❷ This reminds you what has happened prior to the extract.

Macbeth	I have almost forgot the taste of fears; ❸
	The time has been, my senses would have cool'd
	To hear a night-shriek and my fell of hair
	Would at a dismal treatise rouse and stir
	5 As life were in't. I have supp'd full with horrors;
	Direness familiar to my slaughterous thoughts
	Cannot once start me. Wherefore was that cry?
Seyton	The queen, my lord, is dead.
Macbeth	She should have died hereafter;
	10 There would have been a time for such a word.
	Tomorrow, and tomorrow, and tomorrow
	Creeps in this petty pace from day to day
	To the last syllable of recorded time;
	And all our yesterdays have lighted fools
	15 The way to dusty death. Out, out, brief candle,
	Life's but a walking shadow, a poor player
	That struts and frets his hour upon the stage
	And then is heard no more. It is a tale
	Told by an idiot, full of sound and fury
	20 Signifying nothing.

❸ The extract is usually between 20 and 50 lines long.

❹ This reminds you to include comments on the extract.

❺ AO1 trigger – telling you to write in detail, engage with a debate, and give a judgement.

Starting with this speech, ❹ explore how far ❺ Shakespeare presents ❻ Macbeth ❼ as a character you can feel pity for. ❽

Write about:
- how Shakespeare presents Macbeth in this extract ❾
- how Shakespeare presents Macbeth in the play as a whole. ❿

[30 marks]

AO4 [4 marks]

❻ AO2 trigger – alerts you to comment on how structure and language choices are used: the writer's methods.

❼ A key question focus – your response needs to focus on this character.

❽ A key focus and AO3 trigger – inviting you to write about ideas connected with pity in regard to the character.

❾ A reminder that you must include comments on the extract.

❿ A reminder that you must include comments on the rest of the play.

Knowledge 87

# Knowledge EXAM SKILLS

Exam skills

A five-part strategy for tackling the question

1. Start by looking at the question (rather than the extract) and work out what you are being asked to do. Underline key words.
2. Consider the points you will make in your answer – they must be relevant to the question.
3. Think about specific parts of the play you will write about.
4. Look at the extract and identify which parts of it you will write about in your response.
5. Open your response by clearly stating an overall view, and then bring in your points, making sure your comments are developed.

REMEMBER
Be confident about the extract – there will always be something you can use for your answer. Don't expect to always understand everything that's said in the extract, and don't be put off by any words you can't quite work out.

EXAM TIP
Try not to think of the question as 'a question about an extract'. Start by focusing on the question itself and see the extract as a helpful gift that will get you underway and be useful for quotations. Only use bits of the extract that are relevant to the specific question. Don't waste time heavily annotating the extract.

Response structure

A good response presents ideas in a sequence. The best responses start by setting out a view or concept that will be argued over the next few pages. The benefit of starting your response this way is that it immediately signals to an examiner what you are going to be saying, and it also gives a shape to your whole response.

How responses are assessed

Put simply, an examiner is deciding how well you have answered the question.

Examiners mark holistically. This means they read your answer in full and judge it overall awarding a mark out of 30. With the exception of the 4 marks for AO4, they don't award individual marks for each Assessment Objective (even though the published mark scheme illustrates things this way). Instead, they award a mark out of 30 that rewards what you have achieved overall.

As you can see, the more you engage with and show your perceptiveness of the ideas of the text and the methods used, the higher the level you will be awarded.

You don't need to write lots of pages to score highly, but you do need to write enough to show the quality of your understanding. Most successful answers are between three and four sides.

EXAM TIP
There is no precise guide to how much you need to write – it's the quality of your ideas that count – but you're unlikely to score more than half marks if you only write two sides.

Mark scheme levels

Mark scheme level	Mark range out of 30	Typical features of this level
Level 1	1–5	A SIMPLE response • occasional focus on the question • simple points made • little engagement with ideas • little engagement with methods • some misunderstandings • phrasing might be unclear
Level 2	6–10	A RELEVANT response • question focus generally secure • relevant if underdeveloped ideas • generally competent understanding • phrasing mainly clear • some engagement with ideas • basic grasp of methods
Level 3	11–15	An EXPLAINED response • focus on the question secure • points are explained using examples and explanation • competent understanding • phrasing mainly clear • some engagement with ideas • sound grasp of methods
Level 4	16–20	A CLEAR response • focus on the question secure • points are clear and developed • clear and secure understanding • clear phrasing • clear engagement with ideas • clear grasp of methods
Level 5	21–25	A THOUGHTFUL response • focus on the question secure • points are clear and developed with insight • clear and secure understanding with useful details • clear phrasing • clear and thoughtful engagement with ideas • clear grasp of methods
Level 6	26–30	A CONCEPTUAL response • focus on the question secure • points explore ideas at a high level • insightful understanding with useful details • clear/fluent phrasing • perceptive engagement with ideas • perceptive grasp of methods

Knowledge

EXAM SKILLS

Sample answers

Sample answer 1 – Lower level

Here is an extract from a student response to the exam-style question on page 87, with the examiner's annotations and final comments. This response receives less than half marks.

> Explore how far Shakespeare presents Macbeth as a character you can feel pity for.
>
> **[30 marks]**
>
> **AO4 [4 marks]**

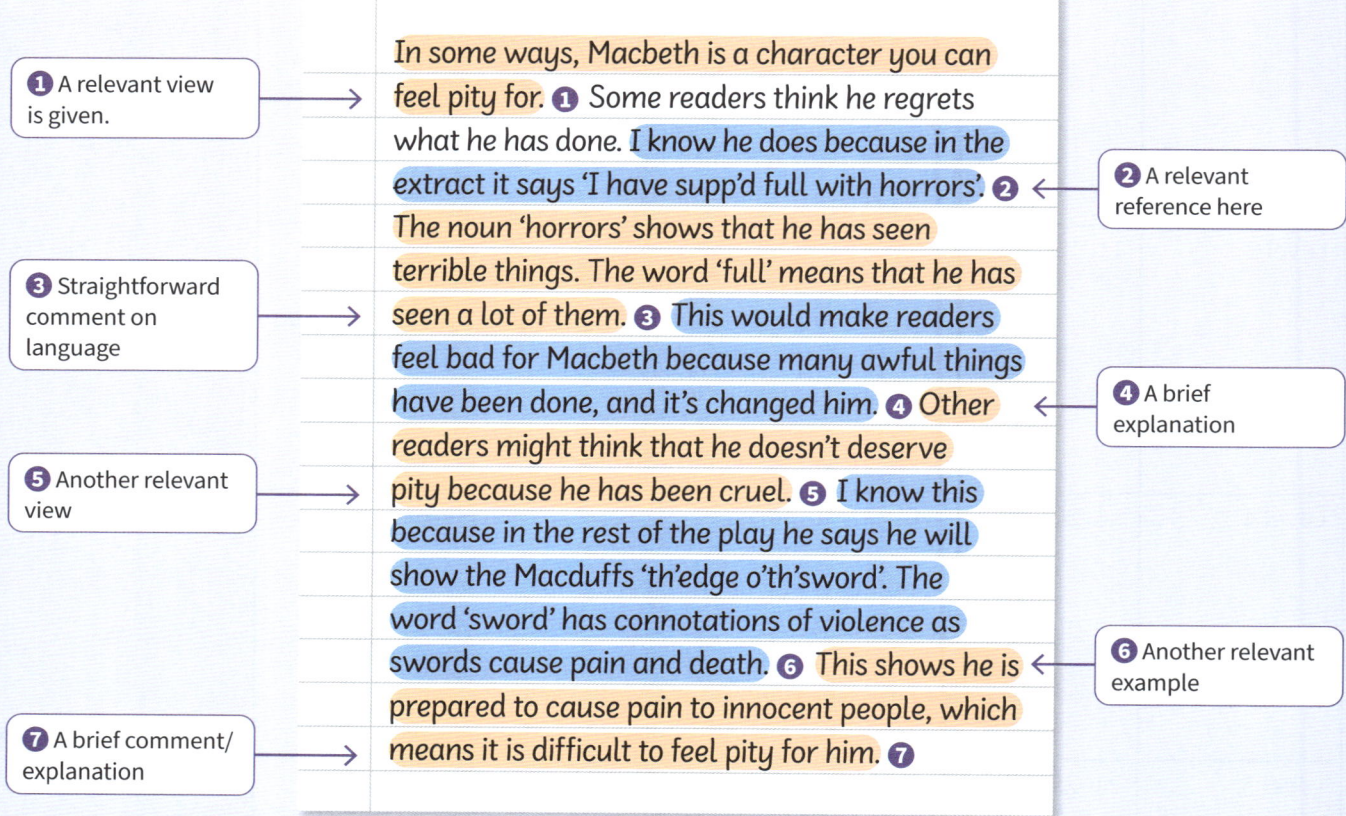

❶ A relevant view is given.

❷ A relevant reference here

❸ Straightforward comment on language

❹ A brief explanation

❺ Another relevant view

❻ Another relevant example

❼ A brief comment/explanation

Student response:

In some ways, Macbeth is a character you can feel pity for. ❶ Some readers think he regrets what he has done. I know he does because in the extract it says 'I have supp'd full with horrors'. ❷ The noun 'horrors' shows that he has seen terrible things. The word 'full' means that he has seen a lot of them. ❸ This would make readers feel bad for Macbeth because many awful things have been done, and it's changed him. ❹ Other readers might think that he doesn't deserve pity because he has been cruel. ❺ I know this because in the rest of the play he says he will show the Macduffs 'th'edge o'th'sword'. The word 'sword' has connotations of violence as swords cause pain and death. ❻ This shows he is prepared to cause pain to innocent people, which means it is difficult to feel pity for him. ❼

Examiner's comments

The response is answering the question in a straightforward way. A 'PEE' structure (Point – Evidence – Explanation) is used. The comments do explain views, but there isn't much development. Comments on language are explained but they aren't very insightful.

> **EXAM TIP**
>
> Paragraph structures such as 'PEE' can be limiting – they can stop you from developing ideas and don't always help you to write conceptually.

Sample answer 2 – Mid level

Here is a student response to the exam-style question on page 87, with the examiner's annotations and final comments. This response receives around half marks.

> Explore how far Shakespeare presents Macbeth as a character you can feel pity for.
>
> [30 marks]
>
> AO4 [4 marks]

❶ Sets out an overall view that will be argued in the response

❸ Sees how method works and touches on the rest of the play

❺ Extends the argument with a further apt reference

Macbeth's journey in the play mainly shows his foolishness and cruelty, but, by the end of the play, his feelings of misery do allow the audience to feel some sense of pity for what he has become. ❶ In the extract, Shakespeare uses Macbeth's dialogue to show that he is a miserable character by the end of the play. He no longer feels much at all, so, when he hears a scream, he reflects that he has 'forgot the taste of fears'. ❷ This contrasts with his earlier feelings about killing Duncan, where he deliberated about it, ❸ and his immediate thoughts after he commits the murder are regret and guilt. Although it's fair to say that he brought it on himself, you can feel some pity for him because he made errors and they have cost him. ❹
The extract also shows that he has become less of a human by the end, and this might cause you to feel pity. For instance, he feels little after his wife's death and comes to realise that life is pointless. ❺ Shakespeare uses metaphors to show what Macbeth thinks about how his attitudes have changed. The idea that life is 'a tale Told by an idiot' and that it is 'signifying nothing' show that he views life as being worthless. Shakespeare seems to be saying that making awful decisions causes people to become less human, so, for this reason, you can pity him. ❻ Any person who thinks life is 'a walking shadow' must be feeling depressed, so the whole speech shows that he is at such a low point that you can pity him.

Continued

❷ Identifies a specific part of the extract

❹ Makes a clear and logical judgement here

❻ A clear, developed comment

Knowledge

EXAM SKILLS

Sample answers

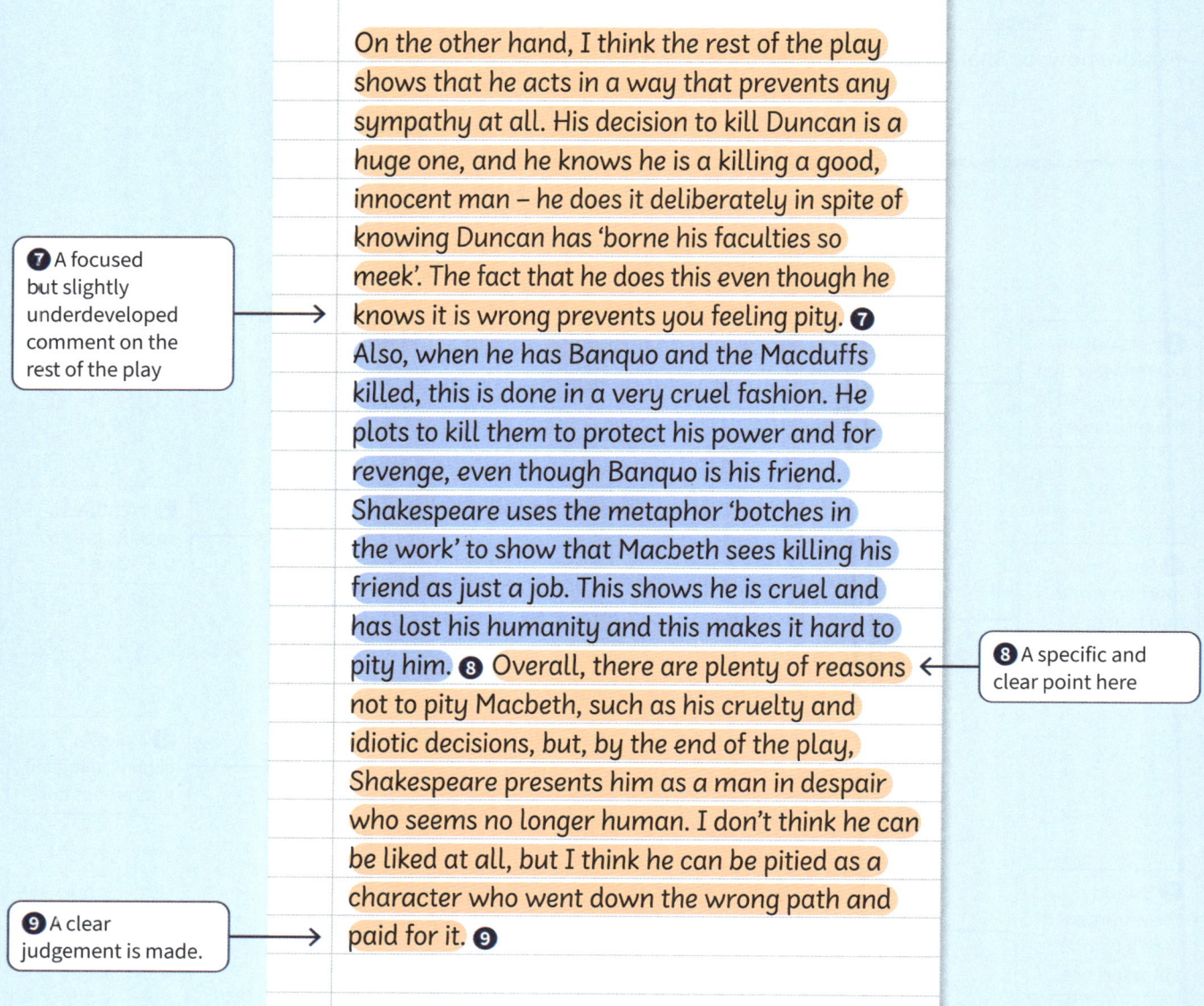

7 A focused but slightly underdeveloped comment on the rest of the play

On the other hand, I think the rest of the play shows that he acts in a way that prevents any sympathy at all. His decision to kill Duncan is a huge one, and he knows he is a killing a good, innocent man – he does it deliberately in spite of knowing Duncan has 'borne his faculties so meek'. The fact that he does this even though he knows it is wrong prevents you feeling pity. **7** Also, when he has Banquo and the Macduffs killed, this is done in a very cruel fashion. He plots to kill them to protect his power and for revenge, even though Banquo is his friend. Shakespeare uses the metaphor 'botches in the work' to show that Macbeth sees killing his friend as just a job. This shows he is cruel and has lost his humanity and this makes it hard to pity him. **8** Overall, there are plenty of reasons not to pity Macbeth, such as his cruelty and idiotic decisions, but, by the end of the play, Shakespeare presents him as a man in despair who seems no longer human. I don't think he can be liked at all, but I think he can be pitied as a character who went down the wrong path and paid for it. **9**

8 A specific and clear point here

9 A clear judgement is made.

Examiner's comments

The question focus is good throughout. The opening statement gives a shape to the response. There is clear focus on the extract with apt references used. Clear and developed comments are made. There is a clear sense of how Shakespeare's methods help to create meanings.

Sample answer 2 – Higher level

Here is a student response to the exam-style question on page 87, with the examiner's annotations and final comments. This response receives high marks.

> Explore how far Shakespeare presents Macbeth as a character you can feel pity for.
>
> [30 marks]
>
> AO4 [4 marks]

In spite of the terrible nature of Macbeth's crimes, audiences can see the catastrophic effect they have upon him – his regret, fear, and ultimate despair make him an object of pity. Shakespeare allows the audience to see the process of Macbeth's tragic downfall; a lot of stage time is given over to observing Macbeth's deliberations about regicide, the way in which he is manipulated, and the terrible effects of his actions upon others and himself. By focusing on the process of his downfall, Shakespeare encourages the audience to pity Macbeth. ❶

In Act 5, Shakespeare shows us a man facing death. In typical tragic fashion, he is forced to confront his errors and what they have made him into. Shakespeare uses dialogue to reveal Macbeth's moment of realisation that he has lost all sense of emotion – he has 'forgot the taste of fears' and knows that his crimes – those horrors he has 'supp'd full' of – have dehumanised him. He feels nothing by the end of his journey, and this is a reason to pity him. ❷ Macbeth is not foolish – he can plainly see how his actions have affected him – and this tragic realisation is a moment of real pity. He knows he has messed up and is made to reflect upon it. The greatest pity is that he can do nothing about it. His fate is inevitable. ❸

Continued

❶ A well-phrased and detailed thesis that sees how methods create pity

❷ Well-chosen references that are discussed in detail

❸ Confident awareness of tragedy here

Knowledge — Exam Skills

Sample answers

Macbeth's nihilistic final soliloquy is also a moment of high pity. His immediate response to his wife's death is not grief but despair at the point he has reached in life. Shakespeare uses multiple instances of figurative language to express the character's despair. The idea that life is just a journey fools take to 'dusty death', and the images of a walking shadow, a bad actor, and a brief candle all suggest a feeling of utter misery. The final image of life as a pointless tale sums up his view that there's nothing to believe in anymore. It's impossible to read these lines and not feel pity. **4** There are many terrible acts that Macbeth commits in the play – the murders of Duncan, Banquo, and the Macduffs are all examples of how his evil acts harm innocent people – but Shakespeare chooses to focus on the internal feelings of Macbeth, which encourages the audience to feel some pity. Tragedy invites the reader to understand why and how people's errors cause their suffering. **5** Shakespeare's play doesn't show the death of Duncan; instead, it shows the heartache of Macbeth and the immediate effects of his first crime. He 'does murder sleep', is appalled by noises, and longs to 'wash this blood' from his hands. Once he has killed Duncan, he is no longer happy or secure. His life becomes a series of violent acts and fear. Although his acts are indefensible, it's impossible not to pity the tragic character he becomes. **6** Macbeth can also be pitied for the foolishness of his decisions. For instance, he recklessly trusts the witches' assertion that he will be safe and will not 'yield To one of woman born'. Shakespeare positions the audience so it can see that the other prophecy regarding Birnam Wood moving is already coming true. This use of dramatic irony creates pity for Macbeth – the audience is watching a man heading to his imminent death, while unaware

4 Another confident, detailed, and well-argued point that has a sharp awareness of method

5 Another well-chosen and expressed conceptual idea

6 Continues with well-argued, deep, and developed ideas here

of it. Although he deserves retribution, the spectacle of a powerful man relying on half-truths does evoke a sense of pity. ⑦ The play itself is a moral lesson in what happens if you allow ambition to go unchecked. It would be impossible to feel pity if Macbeth was simply a monstrous power-seeker, but because Shakespeare commences the play with examples of his bravery – even Duncan calls him a 'worthy gentleman' – the audience sees that he is essentially a good man who makes a terrible set of decisions. Read in this way, his tragic downfall is a cause for pity. ⑧ By the end, he is without 'honour, love, obedience... friends'. He is despised, his wife is dead, and he sees life as futile. His final soliloquy commences with his throwaway remark that his wife 'should have died hereafter'. Although his actions are reprehensible, it is impossible not to feel pity for his despairing belief that life is nothing more than a 'tale Told by an idiot' contrasted with the character seen earlier in the play. It's this gap between what he was and what he has become that allows the reader to extend their pity at the fall of a once greatly respected man. ⑨

⑦ Deals with events in the rest of the play with confidence

⑧ Another detailed point based on the rest of the play

⑨ Concludes with a powerful and convincing judgement

Examiner's comments

This is a fluent and perceptive response. There are several impressive points made to support the overall argument. A very good awareness of how methods are used to bring out meanings is evident. There is a confident handling of concepts, such as tragedy.

REMEMBER

You don't need to refer to named critical opinions or imagine what other readers might think. Giving your own, well-argued opinion is good enough.

Knowledge

Knowledge

EXAM SKILLS

Sample answers

Five key reminders

1. Always keep focused on what the question asks you to do – look at the key words and stick to the question throughout.
2. Choose the most useful parts of the extract and the rest of the play to help you answer the question.
3. Make sure your responses have a 'direction' – set up your views straight away and argue them clearly.
4. Develop your points and comments – sometimes 'saying a bit more' is the key to a better mark.
5. Always link your points to the big ideas of the text – show off your understanding of what the text is 'about'.

> **REMEMBER**
>
> Your understanding of ideas and the deeper points made in the play is the most important aspect of your response, so always make sure this comes through in your writing.

> **EXAM TIP**
>
> There is no requirement to write about the extract first in your response. You can write about the rest of the play first, or weave between the extract and the rest of the play throughout. This latter allows a stronger, thematic response to the question.

Retrieval

Are the following statements true or false? Answer the questions then cover the answers column with a piece of paper and write down as many answers as you can. Check and repeat.

Questions | Answers

#	Question	Answer
1	Learning lots of quotations is the best use of your revision time.	False
2	You must write about historical context.	False
3	Up to 5 marks are awarded for technical accuracy.	False (it is 4 marks)
4	The assessment objectives are embedded in the question.	True
5	You must write about the extract and the rest of the play.	True
6	Examiners award a mark for your whole response.	True
7	There are nine levels in the examiner's mark scheme.	False (there are six)
8	You can only write one side and still do really well.	False
9	Always write about the extract first then the rest of the play.	False
10	You must include named critics in your response.	False

Previous questions

Now go back and use these questions to check your knowledge of previous topics.

Questions | Answers

#	Question	Answer
1	'Out, out, brief candle' Explain what technique is being used here and what it means.	The metaphor underlines the futility Macbeth experiences by the end of the play and shows where his tragic errors have led him
2	Complete the quotation using three words: 'Have pluck'd my nipple from his _____ And _____ the brains out'	'Have pluck'd my nipple from his <u>boneless gums</u> And <u>dash'd</u> the brains out'
3	Which two characters are not deceived by the Macbeths?	Malcolm and Macduff

# Practice

Exam-style questions

Use the questions in this section to practise the knowledge and skills you have learned.

1

Read the following extract from Act 2 Scene 2 of *Macbeth* and then answer the question that follows.

At this point in the play, Macbeth has just killed Duncan and returns to talk to his wife.

EXAM TIP

Remember to begin by planning an answer. Start your thinking by looking at the question first rather than the extract.

Macbeth	I'll go no more.
	I am afraid to think what I have done;
	Look on't again, I dare not.
Lady Macbeth	Infirm of purpose!
5	Give me the daggers. The sleeping and the dead
	Are but as pictures; 'tis the eye of childhood
	That fears a painted devil. If he do bleed,
	I'll gild the faces of the grooms withal,
	For it must seem their guilt. [*Exit*]
10	*Knock within*
Macbeth	Whence is that knocking?
	How is't with me, when every noise appals me?
	What hands are here? Ha: they pluck out mine eyes.
	Will all great Neptune's ocean wash this blood
15	Clean from my hand? No: this my hand will rather
	The multitudinous seas incarnadine,
	Making the green one red.
	Enter Lady Macbeth
Lady Macbeth	My hands are of your colour, but I shame
20	To wear a heart so white.

Starting with this speech, explore how Shakespeare presents Macbeth's feelings about murder.

Write about:

- how Shakespeare presents Macbeth's reaction to Duncan's murder in this extract
- how Shakespeare presents Macbeth's feelings about other murders in the play as a whole.

[30 marks]
AO4 [4 marks]

2

Read the following extract from Act 3 Scene 2 of *Macbeth* and then answer the question that follows.

At this point in the play, Macbeth has killed Duncan and is planning the murders of Banquo and Fleance.

> **Lady Macbeth**   How now, my lord, why do you keep alone,
> Of sorriest fancies your companions making,
> Using those thoughts which should indeed have died
> With them they think on? Things without all remedy
> 5 Should be without regard; what's done, is done.
>
> **Macbeth**   We have scorch'd the snake, not kill'd it;
> She'll close, and be herself, whilst our poor malice
> Remains in danger of her former tooth.
> But let the frame of things disjoint, both the worlds suffer,
> 10 Ere we will eat our meal in fear, and sleep
> In the affliction of these terrible dreams
> That shake us nightly. Better be with the dead
> Whom we, to gain our peace, have sent to peace,
> Than on the torture of the mind to lie
> 15 In restless ecstasy. Duncan is in his grave.
> After life's fitful fever, he sleeps well;
> Treason has done his worst; nor steel nor poison,
> Malice domestic, foreign levy, nothing
> Can touch him further.

EXAM TIP

Look closely at the way each question is set up. Remember that 'how far' questions require a judgement on your part.

Starting with this speech, explore how far Shakespeare presents Macbeth as a character who suffers.

Write about:

- how Shakespeare presents Macbeth in this extract
- how Shakespeare presents Macbeth in the play as a whole.

[30 marks]
AO4 [4 marks]

Practice

Exam-style questions

3

Read the following extract from Act 5 Scene 5 of *Macbeth* and then answer the question that follows.

At this point in the play, Macbeth's castle is surrounded and he has heard a scream.

EXAM TIP

Look for opportunities to write about structure in your response. A question which asks about change directs you to think about how a character develops during the structure of the play.

Macbeth	I have almost forgot the taste of fears;
	The time has been, my senses would have cool'd
	To hear a night-shriek and my fell of hair
	Would at a dismal treatise rouse and stir
5	As life were in't. I have supp'd full with horrors;
	Direness familiar to my slaughterous thoughts
	Cannot once start me. Wherefore was that cry?
Seyton	The queen, my lord, is dead.
Macbeth	She should have died hereafter;
10	There would have been a time for such a word.
	Tomorrow, and tomorrow, and tomorrow
	Creeps in this petty pace from day to day
	To the last syllable of recorded time;
	And all our yesterdays have lighted fools
15	The way to dusty death. Out, out, brief candle,
	Life's but a walking shadow, a poor player
	That struts and frets his hour upon the stage
	And then is heard no more. It is a tale
	Told by an idiot, full of sound and fury
20	Signifying nothing.

Starting with this speech, explore how far Shakespeare presents Macbeth as a character who changes.

Write about:

- how Shakespeare presents Macbeth in this extract
- how Shakespeare presents Macbeth in the play as a whole.

[30 marks]
AO4 [4 marks]

4

Read the following extract from Act 1 Scene 5 of *Macbeth* and then answer the question that follows.

At this point in the play, Lady Macbeth is thinking about the murder of Duncan.

EXAM TIP
Remember that four marks are available for the accuracy of your spelling, punctuation and grammar, so always leave time to re-read your response and check it for errors.

Lady Macbeth   The raven himself is hoarse
That croaks the fatal entrance of Duncan
Under my battlements. Come, you spirits
That tend on mortal thoughts, unsex me here,
5   And fill me from the crown to the toe topfull
Of direst cruelty; make thick my blood,
Stop up th'access and passage to remorse
That no compunctious visitings of nature
Shake my fell purpose nor keep peace between
10   Th'effect and it. Come to my woman's breasts
And take my milk for gall, you murd'ring ministers,
Wherever in your sightless substances
You wait on nature's mischief. Come, thick night,
And pall thee in the dunnest smoke of hell,
15   That my keen knife see not the wound it makes,
Nor heaven peep through the blanket of the dark,
To cry, 'Hold, hold.'

Starting with this speech, explore how far Shakespeare presents Lady Macbeth as an evil character.

Write about:

- how Shakespeare presents Lady Macbeth as an evil character in this speech
- how Shakespeare presents Lady Macbeth as an evil character in the play as a whole.

[30 marks]
AO4 [4 marks]

Practice

Practice

Exam-style questions

5

Read the following extract from Act 1 Scene 5 of *Macbeth* and then answer the question that follows.

At this point in the play, Lady Macbeth has received a letter from her husband telling her of the witches' predictions, and is reflecting on its contents.

> **Lady Macbeth**   Glamis thou art, and Cawdor, and shalt be
> What thou art promis'd; yet do I fear thy nature,
> It is too full o'th'milk of human kindness
> To catch the nearest way. Thou wouldst be great,
> 5   Art not without ambition, but without
> The illness should attend it. What thou wouldst highly,
> That wouldst thou holily; wouldst not play false,
> And yet wouldst wrongly win. Thou'dst have, great Glamis,
> 10   That which cries, 'Thus thou must do' if thou have it;
> And that which rather thou dost fear to do,
> Than wishest should be undone. Hie thee hither,
> That I may pour my spirits in thine ear
> And chastise with the valour of my tongue
> 15   All that impedes thee from the golden round,
> Which fate and metaphysical aid doth seem
> To have thee crown'd withal.

> **EXAM TIP**
>
> When selecting parts from the extract to use, always make sure the lines you choose are directly relevant to the question being asked.

Starting with this speech, explore how far Shakespeare presents Lady Macbeth as a powerful character.

Write about:

- how Shakespeare presents Lady Macbeth in this extract
- how Shakespeare presents Lady Macbeth in the play as a whole.

[30 marks]
AO4 [4 marks]

6

Read the following extract from Act 5 Scene 1 of *Macbeth* and then answer the question that follows.

At this point in the play, a doctor has arrived to treat Lady Macbeth. In the extract, she is talking in her sleep.

Lady Macbeth Out, damned spot! Out, I say! One, two. Why, then, 'tis time to do't. Hell is murky. Fie, my lord, fie, a soldier, and afeard? What need we fear who knows it, when none can call our power to account? Yet who would have thought the old man to have had so much blood in him.

Doctor Do you mark that?

Lady Macbeth The Thane of Fife had a wife. Where is she now? What, will these hands ne'er be clean? No more o'that, my lord, no more o'that. You mar all with this starting.

Doctor Go to, go to; you have known what you should not.

Gentlewoman She has spoke what she should not, I am sure of that Heaven knows what she has known.

Lady Macbeth Here's the smell of the blood still; all the perfumes of Arabia will not sweeten this little hand. O, O, O.

Doctor What a sigh is there! The heart is sorely charged.

Starting with this speech, explore how far Shakespeare presents Lady Macbeth as a character you can feel sympathy with.

Write about:

- how Shakespeare presents Lady Macbeth in this extract
- how Shakespeare presents Lady Macbeth in the play as a whole.

[30 marks]
AO4 [4 marks]

EXAM TIP

Always check which part of the play the extract is taken from. This will help you begin to think about structure, and at which point in the story we are viewing the character from.

Practice

Exam-style questions

7

Read the following extract from Act 3 Scene 2 of *Macbeth* and then answer the question that follows.

At this point in the play, Duncan has been murdered and the Macbeths are preparing for a banquet.

> **Lady Macbeth** Nought's had, all's spent
> Where our desire is got without content.
> 'Tis safer to be that which we destroy
> Than by destruction dwell in doubtful joy.
>
> 5 *Enter* Macbeth
>
> How now, my lord, why do you keep alone,
> Of sorriest fancies your companions making,
> Using those thoughts which should indeed have died
> With them they think on? Things without all remedy
> 10 Should be without regard; what's done is done.
>
> **Macbeth** We have scorch'd the snake, not kill'd it;
> She'll close, and be herself, whilst our poor malice
> Remains in danger of her former tooth.
> But let the frame of things disjoint, both the worlds suffer,
> 15 Ere we will eat our meal in fear and sleep
> In the affliction of these terrible dreams
> That shake us nightly. Better be with the dead
> Whom we, to gain our peace, have sent to peace,
> Than on the torture of the mind to lie
> 20 In restless ecstasy. Duncan is in his grave.
> After life's fitful fever, he sleeps well;
> Treason has done his worst: nor steel nor poison,
> Malice domestic, foreign levy, nothing
> Can touch him further.

> **EXAM TIP**
>
> When answering questions that feature two characters, there is no need to write about them equally, but make sure that you do cover both.

Starting with this speech, explore how far Shakespeare presents Macbeth and Lady Macbeth as unhappy characters.

Write about:

- how Shakespeare presents the Macbeths as unhappy in this extract
- how Shakespeare presents the Macbeths as unhappy in the play as a whole.

[30 marks]
AO4 [4 marks]

8

Read the following extract from Act 1 Scene 3 of *Macbeth* and then answer the question that follows.

At this point in the play, the witches have predicted Macbeth's future.

EXAM TIP

Remember to focus your answer on the big ideas and themes that relate to the question. Always try to write in detail and show off the quality of your thinking in relation to the idea in the question.

Macbeth	[*Aside*] Two truths are told,
	As happy prologues to the swelling act
	Of the imperial theme.—I thank you, gentlemen.—
	This supernatural soliciting
5	Cannot be ill, cannot be good. If ill,
	Why hath it given me earnest of success,
	Commencing in a truth? I am Thane of Cawdor.
	If good, why do I yield to that suggestion,
	Whose horrid image doth unfix my hair
10	And make my seated heart knock at my ribs
	Against the use of nature? Present fears
	Are less than horrible imaginings.
	My thought, whose murder yet is but fantastical,
	Shakes so my single state of man that function
15	Is smother'd in surmise, and nothing is,
	But what is not.
Banquo	Look how our partner's rapt.
Macbeth	If chance will have me king, why chance may crown me
	Without my stir.

Starting with this speech, explore how Shakespeare presents ideas about ambition.

Write about:

- how Shakespeare presents ideas about ambition in this extract
- how Shakespeare presents ideas about ambition in the play as a whole.

[30 marks]
AO4 [4 marks]

Practice

Exam-style questions

9

Read the following extract from Act 5 Scene 9 of *Macbeth* and then answer the question that follows.

At this point in the play, Macbeth has been killed and Malcolm declared king.

Malcolm   We shall not spend a large expense of time
                Before we reckon with your several loves
                And make us even with you. My thanes and kinsmen,
                Henceforth be earls, the first that ever Scotland
            5   In such an honour nam'd. What's more to do
                Which would be planted newly with the time,—
                As calling home our exil'd friends abroad
                That fled the snares of watchful tyranny,
                Producing forth the cruel ministers
           10   Of this dead butcher and his fiend-like queen,
                Who, as 'tis thought, by self and violent hands
                Took off her life,—this and what needful else
                That calls upon us, by the grace of Grace
                We will perform in measure, time, and place.
           15   So, thanks to all at once and to each one,
                Whom we invite to see us crown'd at Scone.

Starting with this speech, explore how Shakespeare presents attitudes to being king.

Write about:
- how Shakespeare presents King Malcolm in this extract
- how Shakespeare presents kings in the play as a whole.

[30 marks]
AO4 [4 marks]

> **EXAM TIP**
> Don't be put off if the extract is one you are less familiar with. Remember that it is the question that is most important, so look for parts of the extract that link directly to the question and start with those.

10

Read the following extract from Act 4 Scene 3 of *Macbeth* and then answer the question that follows.

At this point in the play, Macbeth has killed Macduff's family.

Macduff		He has no children. All my pretty ones?
		Did you say all? O hell-kite! All?
		What, all my pretty chickens and their dam
		At one fell swoop?
Malcolm	5	Dispute it like a man.
Macduff		I shall do so;
		But I must also feel it as a man;
		I cannot but remember such things were
		That were most precious to me. Did heaven look on,
	10	And would not take their part? Sinful Macduff,
		They were all struck for thee. Naught that I am,
		Not for their own demerits but for mine,
		Fell slaughter on their souls. Heaven rest them now.
Malcolm		Be this the whetstone of your sword, let grief
	15	Convert to anger. Blunt not the heart, enrage it.
Macduff		O, I could play the woman with mine eyes
		And braggart with my tongue. But gentle heavens,
		Cut short all intermission. Front to front
		Bring thou this fiend of Scotland and myself;
	20	Within my sword's length set him. If he scape,
		Heaven forgive him too.

EXAM TIP

When planning an answer, you might find that there are lots of points you could make. Choose the most impressive ideas and write about those in detail, rather than trying to cover every point.

Starting with this speech, explore how Shakespeare presents ideas about death.

Write about:

- how Shakespeare presents death in this extract
- how Shakespeare presents death in the play as a whole.

[30 marks]
AO4 [4 marks]

Practice

Exam-style questions

11

Read the following extract from Act 2 Scene 2 of *Macbeth* and then answer the question that follows.

At this point in the play, Macbeth has killed Duncan.

Macbeth	I'll go no more. I am afraid to think what I have done; Look on't again, I dare not.
Lady Macbeth	Infirm of purpose! 5 Give me the daggers. The sleeping and the dead Are but as pictures; 'tis the eye of childhood That fears a painted devil. If he do bleed, I'll gild the faces of the grooms withal, For it must seem their guilt. *[Exit*
	10 *Knock within*
Macbeth	Whence is that knocking? How is't with me, when every noise appals me? What hands are here? Ha: they pluck out mine eyes. Will all great Neptune's ocean wash this blood 15 Clean from my hand? No: this my hand will rather The multitudinous seas incarnadine, Making the green one red.

> **EXAM TIP**
>
> Where extracts feature two central characters, look at each character's attitudes to the key term in the question. Often, these characters have conflicting attitudes.

Starting with this speech, explore how Shakespeare presents feelings about murder.

Write about:

- how Shakespeare presents feelings about murder in this extract
- how Shakespeare presents feelings about murder in the play as a whole.

[30 marks]
AO4 [4 marks]

12

Read the following extract from Act 1 Scene 5 of *Macbeth* and then answer the question that follows.

At this point in the play, the Macbeths are discussing murdering Duncan.

Macbeth	My dearest love, Duncan comes here tonight.
Lady Macbeth	And when goes hence?
Macbeth	Tomorrow, as he purposes.
Lady Macbeth 5	O never Shall sun that morrow see. Your face, my thane, is as a book where men May read strange matters. To beguile the time, Look like the time, bear welcome in your eye, 10 Your hand, your tongue; look like th'innocent flower, But be the serpent under't. He that's coming Must be provided for, and you shall put This night's great business into my dispatch, Which shall to all our nights and days to come 15 Give solely sovereign sway and masterdom.

> **EXAM TIP**
> Remember that the key term in a question has a variety of synonyms and these can help you develop ideas. For example, a question about deception should prompt you to think about lies, betrayal and treachery.

Starting with this speech, explore how Shakespeare presents ideas about deception.

Write about:

- how Shakespeare presents deception in this extract
- how Shakespeare presents deception in the play as a whole.

[30 marks]
AO4 [4 marks]

Practice

Exam-style questions

13

Read the following extract from Act 2 Scene 2 of *Macbeth* and then answer the question that follows.

At this point in the play, Macbeth has murdered Duncan.

Macbeth	But wherefore could not I pronounce 'Amen'?
	I had most need of blessing and 'Amen'
	Stuck in my throat.
Lady Macbeth	These deeds must not be thought
5	After these ways; so, it will make us mad.
Macbeth	Methought I heard a voice cry, 'Sleep no more:
	Macbeth does murder sleep', the innocent sleep,
	Sleep that knits up the ravell'd sleeve of care,
	The death of each day's life, sore labour's bath,
10	Balm of hurt minds, great nature's second course,
	Chief nourisher in life's feast.
Lady Macbeth	What do you mean?
Macbeth	Still it cried, 'Sleep no more' to all the house;
	'Glamis hath murder'd sleep', and therefore Cawdor
15	Shall sleep no more: Macbeth shall sleep no more
Lady Macbeth	Who was it, that thus cried? Why, worthy thane,
	You do unbend your noble strength to think
	So brain-sickly of things. Go get some water
	And wash this filthy witness from your hand.

Starting with this speech, explore how Shakespeare presents ideas about guilt.

Write about:

- how Shakespeare presents guilt in this extract
- how Shakespeare presents guilt in the play as a whole.

[30 marks]
AO4 [4 marks]

> **EXAM TIP**
>
> Remember that ideas and attitudes towards concepts such as guilt change during the course of the play. Track the way in which the attitudes of the main characters change and what this tells you about the character.

14

Read the following extract from Act 3 Scene 1 of *Macbeth* and then answer the question that follows.

At this point in the play, Macbeth is plotting the deaths of Banquo and Fleance.

Second Murderer	We shall, my lord, Perform what you command us.
First Murderer	Though our lives—
Macbeth	Your spirits shine through you. Within this hour at most, 5 I will advise you where to plant yourselves, Acquaint you with the perfect spy o'th'time, The moment on't, for't must be done tonight, And something from the palace: always thought, That I require a clearness. And with him, 10 To leave no rubs nor botches in the work, Fleance, his son that keeps him company, Whose absence is no less material to me Than is his father's, must embrace the fate Of that dark hour. Resolve yourselves apart, 15 I'll come to you anon.
Murderers	We are resolv'd, my lord.

EXAM TIP

When dealing with a question about ideas such as evil, it can help to start by considering what the ending of the play shows about this idea – in this case, you would consider Shakespeare's final message about evil.

Starting with this speech, explore how Shakespeare presents evil thoughts and actions.

Write about:

- how Shakespeare presents evil thoughts and actions in this extract
- how Shakespeare presents evil thoughts and actions in the play as a whole.

[30 marks]
AO4 [4 marks]

Practice

Exam-style questions

15

Read the following extract from Act 4 Scene 1 of *Macbeth* and then answer the question that follows.

At this point in the play, Macbeth visits the witches to ask about the future.

Thunder. Enter Third Apparition, *a Child crowned with a tree in his hand*

Macbeth	What is this,
	That rises like the issue of a king
5	And wears upon his baby-brow the round
	And top of sovereignty?
All the Witches	Listen, but speak not to't.
Third Apparition	Be lion-mettl'd, proud, and take no care
	Who chafes, who frets, or where conspirers are.
10	Macbeth shall never vanquish'd be until
	Great Birnam Wood to high Dunsinane Hill
	Shall come against him. [*Descends*]
Macbeth	That will never be
	Who can impress the forest, bid the tree
15	Unfix his earthbound root? Sweet bodements, good.
	Rebellious dead, rise never till the wood
	Of Birnam rise, and our high-plac'd Macbeth
	Shall live the lease of nature, pay his breath
	To time and mortal custom. Yet my heart
20	Throbs to know one thing. Tell me, if your art
	Can tell so much, shall Banquo's issue ever
	Reign in this kingdom?
All the Witches	Seek to know no more.

> **EXAM TIP**
>
> A question about the supernatural in the play requires you to decide whether the ghost of Banquo and the dagger are supernatural or products of Macbeth's imagination. Make it clear in your response how you view these entities.

Starting with this speech, explore how Shakespeare presents the power of the supernatural.

Write about:

- how Shakespeare presents the power of the supernatural in this extract
- how Shakespeare presents the power of the supernatural in the play as a whole.

[30 marks]
AO4 [4 marks]

Great Clarendon Street, Oxford, OX2 6DP, United Kingdom

Oxford University Press is a department of the University of Oxford. It furthers the University's objective of excellence in research, scholarship, and education by publishing worldwide. Oxford is a registered trade mark of Oxford University Press in the UK and in certain other countries.

© Oxford University Press 2025

Written by Graham Elsdon
Series editor: Lyndsay Bawden

The moral rights of the authors have been asserted

First published in 2025

All rights reserved. No part of this publication may be reproduced, stored in a retrieval system, transmitted, used for text and data mining, or used for training artificial intelligence, in any form or by any means, without the prior permission in writing of Oxford University Press, or as expressly permitted by law, by licence or under terms agreed with the appropriate reprographics rights organization. Enquiries concerning reproduction outside the scope of the above should be sent to the Rights Department, Oxford University Press, at the address above.

You must not circulate this work in any other form and you must impose this same condition on any acquirer

British Library Cataloguing in Publication Data

Data available

978-1-382-06752-2

978-1-382-06751-5 (ebook)

10 9 8 7 6 5 4 3 2 1

The manufacturing process conforms to the environmental regulations of the country of origin.

Printed in the UK by Bell & Bain.

The manufacturer's authorised representative in the EU for product safety is Oxford University Press España S.A. of el Parque Empresarial San Fernando de Henares, Avenida de Castilla, 2 – 28850 Madrid (www.oup.es/en or product.safety@oup.com). OUP España S.A. also acts as importer into Spain of products made by the manufacturer.

Acknowledgements

The publisher would like to thank Jade Hickin and Sarah Cottinghatt for sharing their expertise and feedback in the development of this resource.

Extracts are from *Oxford School Shakespeare: Macbeth* (Oxford University Press, 2009).

Although we have made every effort to trace and contact all copyright holders before publication this has not been possible in all cases. If notified, the publisher will rectify any errors or omissions at the earliest opportunity.